Online Marketing Success Stories

Insider Secrets From the Experts Who Are Making Millions on the Internet Today

By Rene' V. Richards

Online Marketing Success Stories

Insider Secrets From the Experts Who Are Making Millions on the Internet Today

Copyright © 2006 by Atlantic Publishing Group, Inc.

1210 SW 23rd Place • Ocala, Florida 34474 • 800-814-1132 • 352-622-5836–Fax

Web site: www.atlantic-pub.com • E-mail sales@atlantic-pub.com

SAN Number: 268-1250

ISBN-13: 978-0-910627-65-8   ISBN-10: 0-910627-65-7

Library of Congress Cataloging-in-Publication Data

Richards, Rene' V., 1965-

  Online marketing success stories : insider secrets from the experts who are making millions on the internet today / author, Rene' V. Richards.

       p. cm.

  Includes bibliographical references and index.

  ISBN-13: 978-0-910627-65-8 (alk. paper)

  ISBN-10: 0-910627-65-7

  1. Internet marketing. 2. Internet marketing--Handbooks, manuals, etc. 3. Electronic commerce. 4. Success in business. I. Title.

  HF5415.1265.R525 2006

  658.8'72--dc22

                              2006022894

EDITOR: Marie Lujanac • mlujanac817@yahoo.com

ART DIRECTION: Meg Buchner • megadesn@mchsi.com

BOOK PRODUCTION DESIGN: Laura Siitari of Siitari by Design • www.siitari-design.com

Printed in the United States

TABLE OF CONTENTS

FOREWORD

Online marketing strategies abound and "how to" guides fill our bookshelves. The advice is as inconsistent and contradictory as "how to get rich quick" schemes. There is no single formula or magic recipe for online marketing success. If there were, everyone would use that formula! The average annual income of a small business using the Internet is $3 million per year and U.S. online retail sales will grow from $40.4 billion in 2002 to an estimated $112.5 billion in 2006. There are 2.3 million small companies in the United States with 16 percent of these in the retail trade, and 60 percent of all small companies have an online presence including a Web site. Online shopping or e-commerce has grown from $66 million in 2001 to $132 million 2006.

The truth is that there is no magic formula for success, but the potential for a successful and profitable online business venture grows exponentially each year. Despite the continued growth of the Internet at an unprecedented pace and the growing pool of "experts" claiming to be able to get you the #1 rankings in top search engines and promising other impossible-to-believe claims, there are definite, proven methods, approaches, and techniques to maximize your opportunity for extraordinary success and profitability. They must be correctly interpreted, analyzed, and implemented within your particular industry or market segment.

These proven formulas for success are contained within "Online Marketing Success Stories."

Rene' V. Richards compiles the most comprehensive, user-friendly, and information-rich collection of actual online marketing success strategies, techniques, tips, hints, and case studies ever assembled. This book details experiences from the experts who succeeded in implementing a variety of techniques across a wide-range of market segments with astounding success. Delving deeper into the success stories and marketing strategies, she extracts highly detailed information that can be adapted readily to any successful online marketing campaigns.

This book cuts across a wide variety of successful online marketing campaigns including industry giants such as Microsoft and Google, as well as dozens of individual and small-business success stories. Each is packed with all the strategies, business styles, and industry secrets to propel your online endeavor to success. "Online Marketing Success Stories" is the only publication of its kind that provides implementation guides to integrate these techniques into your own online business venture. It also focuses on a vast amount of technical requirements for successful online Web site development, deployment, and visibility within search engines.

There are dozens of other books that present theory of online marketing techniques, but not one is as comprehensive and informative as Rene' V. Richards's publication "Online Marketing Success Stories," and no other book captures the essential stories behind some of the current online industry leaders. By providing entry into the paths of founders and CEOs of the most successful companies on the World Wide Web today, the author ensures that you will acquire the knowledge that charted the course to success of these companies when thousands of others failed.

Bruce C. Brown, Gizmo Graphics Web Design
Land O Lakes, Florida
Author of *How to Use the Internet to Advertise, Promote and Market Your Business or Web site with Little or No Money*

SECTION ONE

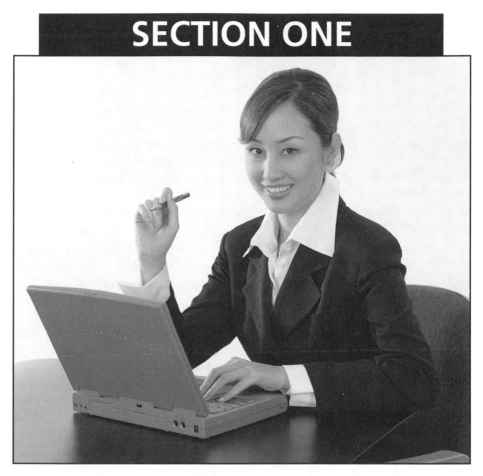

The Real Truth About Success

CHAPTER 1

Internet Information and Research

SUCCESS STORIES

I n this first set of Success Stories, we've included examples of businesses on the Internet that provide search engines, research tools, and materials, information for sale, and industrial research/statistical reports. Almost anything of informational value that can be sold or extracted is the focus of the first set of stories. After all, these are some of the tools you will need to begin your online business. So read on for real opportunity via the Internet.

Mamma Media

![mamma The Mother of All Search Engines]	**Name of company:** Mamma Media
	Date started: July 1996
	Web site: www.mamma.com
	Associate companies: www.copernic.com, www.mammamediasolutions.com, www.mammahealth.com
	E-mail address: deborah@ mamma.com

In July 1996 a new type of Web site was launched when Mamma. com, dubbed the mother of all search engines, hit the Internet. Herman Tumurcuoglu developed it for a master's thesis at Ottawa's Carleton University. It was one of the Web's first search engines to use metasearch technology, and word-of-mouth recommendations brought more visitors to the site. Soon Tumurcuoglu had a handful of people working with him, and they turned the search engine into a source of income by selling banners and licensing its technology to other Web sites.

What exactly is metasearch? When you search for a subject in a metasearch engine it's like using several search engines at once. The metasearch engine searches other content sites and search engines for your topic; it eliminates duplicates, sorts topics by relevance, and provides uniform results. Then they are displayed for you, the consumer. This process gives customers a view of all of the top results from a variety of locations, offering more information than a regular search engine.

As someone who is trying to succeed in online marketing, you should take advantage of any products that could save you time. By using a metasearch engine, like Mamma.com, you will obtain many unique listings and the most trusted results online. You may see fewer results, but they will be more relevant to your topic search. Some examples of metasearch engines are Mamma, **www.mamma.com**; Copernic, **www.copernic.com**; and Dogpile, **www.dogpile.com**.

Mamma.com continued to add in key teams and divisions, expanding the company even further. In November 1999, Intasys Corporation invested $25 million and took 69 percent ownership of Mamma. Then they started an intensive advertising campaign including television commercials and billboards in New York's Times Square.

Noting that there was value in sales of search engine result rankings, Mamma's development team implemented the Premium Search Result Placement Program where advertisers are included in the metasearch results. This program is successful because Mamma doesn't reveal the advertiser's cost-per-click as bid-engines do. As an Internet marketer, you will find this practice beneficial to your own business.

But it's the ranking algorithm that really sets it above competition and gives users an additional benefit. The technology used by Mamma.com is called rSort, and it works like a voting system. When you do a search at Mamma, it queries several engines, and quite often presents duplicate results. At Mamma, the duplicates aren't deleted but instead are ranked depending on the number of "votes" the listing receives. Each duplicate is considered one vote, and the results that have the highest votes end up at the top of the page, making it difficult for SPAMmers to get a top ranking on a metasearch engine, even if they have obtained a high ranking on a regular search engine, which in turn, points you, the Internet marketer, to more legitimate search results.

After going through tremendous growth and the complete buyout by Intasys Corporation, Mamma continues to improve with sophisticated products and services that are beneficial to Internet marketers, such as pay-per-click services, advertising avenues, and exceptional rankings. Mamma keeps its customers and advertisers in mind with the development of each new product. If you haven't taken the time to visit Mamma.com, it is highly recommended that you check out this unique and productive metasearch engine.

Lillian Cauldwell

Name of the company:
Lillian's SpeakOut!

Date started: November 22, 2005

Address: P.O. Box 2344
Ann Arbor, MI 48106-2344

Web site: www.lilliancauldwell.com

Associate companies:
www.smallbusinessreferralnetwork.
com/chapters/?site=MI
www.pvawl.samsbusiness.com
www.authorsden.com/lilliancauldwell

E-mail address: lillian@
lilliancauldwell.com

Lillian Cauldwell is an author, poet, book reviewer, a mentor to teen authors, a speaker, a PodCast media broadcaster, media trainer and the CEO/President of Passionate Voices Around the World Live, an Internet, world wide, public talk, broadcast 24/7, radio station.

Her first nonfiction book was *Teenagers! A Bewildered Parent's Guide*, printed in 1996 by Silvercat Publications, and her recent release, printed in 2003, is an alternate history, science fiction book, *Sacred Honor*, which is set against the early part of the American Revolution, from 1774 to 1776, and against the bitter turmoil of a dying British Empire in 2276.

Lillian was involved in several seminars at Lakeland Community College, Polaris Vocational School, and the Beachwood Library in Cleveland, Ohio. She wrote articles for *The Cleveland Plain Dealer* about a temporary worker's first day, and it was later reprinted in *TempDigest*, a magazine targeting temporary agencies.

Since 1996, Lillian has given local seminars at Lakeland Community College and to professional temporaries. She was invited to speak at several science fiction and fantasy conventions. At present, she is concentrating on submitting her paranormal, mystery novel for "tweens," *The Alpha Mystery – The Lost Gold of Chennault Plantation*. She also teaches two writing classes for "The Long Story Short: Blending History with Fiction" and "Before and After Book Promotion and Marketing."The following is an account of her unique experience with Internet success and the resources she used to fuel her success.

I started hosting an Internet radio talk show called The Lillian Cauldwell Show *with "Artist First Worldwide Radio." After a year, I left and joined "Global Talk Radio." Four months later, I decided to start my own media company, Lillian's SpeakOut! Podcast Media BroadCast Service. In the spring, I'll start broadcasting my own Internet Radio Station called "Passionate Voices Around the World Live" with live talk and hosted programming.*

I knew I could do what I paid other Internet radio stations to do for me. I did my homework (keyword research) and gathered the information. When I was ready, I wrote up a business plan for both businesses: "Lillian's SpeakOut!" and "Passionate Voices Around the World Live."

I knew that I could provide a unique niche product, something that no one else was doing with an Internet radio station. I proposed doing an Internet Radio Station that included live programming with talk show and business hosts, educational classes, seminars, teleseminars, book clubs, forums, book reviews, training, "tween" and teen programming on the weekend to include controversial subjects no one else would do: lesbian programming, religion, politics (local, regional, national, and international), inspiration, world culture, evolution, archaeology, languages, new bands and song-writer wannabes, ministries, threads, conversational poetry, novel excerpts, nonfiction, self-publishing, public relations agents, streaming video, and TiVo, PodCasting. I would interview anyone who had something to say or to teach anyone who never had the opportunity to do so until now. I consider "Passionate Voices Around the World" a challenge for those people whose voices have never been heard because they've never been asked, were afraid to do so because no one would listen, or for those who wrote or called in but never were answered.

There are some key elements to success, that no matter what your area of expertise or your niche market, you must be prepared to address. The following is Lillian's list of the most important, along with some key advice for individuals interested in starting their own online business.

- *Discipline*
- *Responsibility*
- *Teamwork*
- *Delegation*
- *Networking*
- *Cold calling*
- *Research*
- *Dedicated and loyal support personnel*
- *A silent partner (hubby)*
- *Setting priorities*

What is her best advice?

- *Do your homework first.*
- *Check out your competition and see how they're doing it.*
- *Ask questions.*
- *Write a business plan.*

- *Build a foundation.*

- *Build a mailing list of contacts.*

- *Network, Network, Network.*

- *Write articles and/or newsletter.*

- *Become a member of forums relative to your business.*

Lillian's most important piece of advice?

Make sure you are well-funded. Capital, or money, is your biggest need.

Rosalind Gardner

Name: Rosalind Gardner
Web site: rosalindgardner.com
Associate companies:
www.superaffiliatehandbook.com
www.'NetProfitsToday.com

In January 1997 Rosalind Gardner received her first "Web check" and hasn't looked back since. She traded her career as an air traffic controller for full-time 'netpreneurship in early 2000, and her various Internet projects now entertain and inform millions of visitors annually while netting a high six-figure personal income. When asked what she enjoys most about making a living online from home, her answer is "Having the freedom to do what I want, when I want!" She offers this site with you in mind, knowing that if she can earn a good living online you can too.

Rosalind's story is one of real success and doing what she enjoys while making money. In 1998, she was working as an air traffic controller in Canada. The crazy, inhumane shift schedule was literally making her sick, so she had to find some way to replace her income. Fortunately, right around the time she fell ill, she also got connected to the 'Net. It didn't take her long to see the potential for a fun and lucrative home-based business.

Two years after she started to "play" with Web sites, she quit her job as an air traffic controller. Actually, she replaced her income the first year, but wanted to make darned sure that the new business was going to stick. That makes her living proof that anyone can succeed with an Internet business using affiliate programs.

Rosalind's first move was to find a product that filled a need. She settled on a dating site called Sage-Hearts, **www.Sage-Hearts. com**. Here you can find reviews of hundreds of dating sites with an invitation to try the one that suits you and your lifestyle. When visitors join, Rosalind earns a commission from her sponsor.

Rosalind not only earns commissions from her visitors she also gains subscribers for her newsletter ensuring that her visitors will not be lost but will join her business list and become her loyal customers for years to come.

Based on her amazing success as a super affiliate, Rosalind has written the Super Affiliates Handbook with many useful tips and information about making a real living from affiliate programs.

Rosalind attributes her success to several personal characteristics, but she believes anyone can succeed with the following personal elements:

Her determination to succeed: she persevered and built on her successes in this order.

- She found an extremely hot niche in which to work. Dating throughout the ages has enjoyed immense popularity.

- She built a targeted business list with her free newsletter. This allowed her to capture good responsive prospects for her programs and build her business as well as supplying customers to her sponsors.

- She built a theme Web site for her dating niche market and was able to work many affiliate programs from one Web site.

- She is always ready to help others and has built respect and trust for herself. These qualities bring in more business.

- She attracts highly targeted visitors to her site. To drive traffic to her site, Rosalind buys targeted, keyword-specific ads from Google and Overture, which get displayed on the Web's most popular sites, including Yahoo!, AOL, and MSN. This type of advertising means she only spends money when interested people are actively searching for dating information and go to her Web site.

Here's what she lists as the most important objectives when growing your business:

- *Keep it simple.*

- *Don't get slowed down by creating the product yourself.*

- *Add your own unique value to the process. Hers are her reviews and newsletter.*

- *Only invest in performance-based advertising.*

- *Go the extra mile.*

Rosalind offered free updates, articles, and tips to her growing list to help her business grow much faster than those of affiliates who just "hand off" to the merchant Web site. By building her list, she can bring visitors back to her site or send them to other sites through her affiliate link without having to pay for them again.

Harvey Segal

Harvey Segal lives in London with his wife, Sue, and 15-year old daughter, Naomi. He started his online marketing business in 1997 after a career in IT, first in programming, then management. His first site, Super Tips, **www.supertips.com**, was created to provide resources and tips for the online marketer. As such sites became more common and competitive, he decided to focus on niche areas and developed his two popular information sites, The Complete Guide to Ad Tracking Programs, **www.ad-tracking.com** and The Complete Guide to ClickBank, **www.clickbankguide. com**. He produced his first eBook *Guru Magic*, **www.supertips. com/gurus,** when he persuaded more than 35 Internet marketing experts to reveal their top tips. Then he went on to produce his SuperTips series of eBooks:

- AdTracking SuperTips, **www.ad-tracking.com/adbook.html**

- ClickBank Affiliate SuperTips, **www.clickbankguide. com**

- Forum SuperTips, **www.supertips.com/forums**

- 101 SuperTips, **www.supertips.com/101/index.htm**

These are all free books, but they have a viral (word of mouth) element as they can be re-branded with affiliate links. You can find links to all of his books and sites at SuperTips.

Harvey offered this insight into the success of Internet commerce and his experiences.

Since starting online in 1997, I've found that the best method for making money on the 'Net is to focus on a small, specialized area—a niche. The power of viral marketing that I use is to give away free books, which can be re-branded with affiliate links. Free books and viral marketing are a powerful way to promote any business. Focus on a narrow topic or try an unusual idea. Internet marketing is too broad and popular a subject to accommodate yet another site, but the idea of collecting tips from the experts will pay off - and can be extended to any field.

Michael Green

Name: Michael Green
E-mail: Michael@howtocorp.com

Michael Green (pen name) is a 37-year-old Brit living in London. He opened a printing business at 21. Today that business offers design, print, and Web site development services resulting in millions of dollars in sales.

Nowadays, Michael is heavily involved in public service through elected office, but in his spare time before being elected, he developed **www.howtocorp.com** (more on that below). He writes under the pseudonym "Michael Green" to avoid confusion for anyone searching for political comment.

He discovered that his offline experiences helped make him an overnight online success, and the facts speak for themselves. He established his online enterprise only as recently as the spring of 2002, yet today he has created more than 20 toolkit products that are marketed and sold worldwide via the Internet.

He has achieved a constant Top Ten position in the much coveted ClickBank Marketplace, which lists literally tens of thousands of other online products, so the chances are that by the time you've finished reading this biography, he will have made yet more Internet-based sales!

His online business was started with great excitement and a moment of "entrepreneurial seizure." If that's double-dutch then be sure to read the e-myth book by Gerber. He started HowToCorp in April 2002.

His first product was **www.howtoWRITEaNEWSLETTER.com** — quickly followed by **www.EasyEzineToolkit.com** and dozens of others, located at **www.howtocorp.com**. We asked him what he felt he personally brought to the success of his business.

Determination and tenacity. It is really important to have a very clear goal and to keep striving toward that goal. Don't be knocked off course by everyday distractions, big or small. Keep focused and avoid being pulled in too many directions. Most of all don't get sucked into reading everyone else's information and achieving nothing yourself. You should follow only one "guru" at a time!

If you are trying to make money via Internet marketing, you are not alone. There are tens of thousands of folks working on the Internet, trying to generate enough income to leave their "nine-to-five" and live off their online income for good. But sadly, for most of these people, the reality is that they will probably scrape by month-by-month, earning the odd commission check, but never really breaking through to the "Online Big Time"!

Now as someone who has been fortunate enough to translate that ultimate dream of making enough money "while I sleep" to giving up my day job if I chose to, I've been troubled about why others work just as hard as I do (or harder) online but never seem to make it to the holy grail of Internet profits.

So eventually I conducted a piece of research using the responses from people who have taken my Internet marketing mini-course. The results were most revealing—too many experts—too little time!

Something that I had long suspected and have even experienced for myself turns out to be absolutely true. There is a lot of excellent help and advice available for online marketers. You don't need to look very far and you'll soon be stumbling across Internet marketing experts who'll tell you much about important subjects like:

- *Product creation*
- *Autoresponders*
- *Opt-in lists*
- *Follow-up marketing*
- *Choosing the right pricing*
- *Running affiliate programs*

Confusingly, these "experts" set themselves up to be authoritative gurus. And now suddenly for the average Joe trying to make a good living online, the advice marketplace is overcrowded and very confusing. Worse still—one expert seems to be contradicting the next and everyone is shouting so loud that you just don't know where to start. Sure, a lot of the available information seems to be very good, but whom should you believe?

And the result of all this? Complete paralysis!

Your online work lacks direction. One minute you're following guru "A"; next you're dipping into guru "B's" advice; but then an e-mail pops through from guru "S" and what they have to say looks simply irresistible. Suddenly you are being pulled in so many directions that you just can't think.

One Guru at a Time, Please!

So what should you be doing to build your own successful online business? For me and for those I have tutored the answer has been to select one "all-round expert" to follow. Find a marketing mentor whom you feel comfortable with, someone you've read a little about and who you believe can educate you in the rights and wrongs of online product creation and marketing. Most important, take a look at the writing style of the guru you are thinking of following. Ask yourself is this a writing style that I can understand? Does this person have a natural ability to put information across to me in a clear and readable fashion? Most important of all, has this so-called "guru" really done this for themselves? Or to put it another way—do they know what they're talking about?

Now focus on this one person until you've achieved online success. Having answered the above questions and chosen your expert, follow that person until you have become successful yourself. If you've chosen wisely and purchased some of your guru's information, they shouldn't mind if you ask them an occasional direct question.

For example, I frequently receive e-mails like this one: "Michael, I read what you said about XYZ7, but could you point me in the right direction to achieve this other important challenge?" Follow a knowledgeable expert, and they won't mind sharing a little extra information with you. Best of all if you concentrate on one person's advice at a time, you are far more likely to make a success of your own online business—if only because you won't waste your time trying out a little bit from everyone and being pulled in so many directions that you end up achieving nothing.

Willie Crawford

Name: Willie Crawford

E-mail: willie3-56875@autocontactor.com

I'm telling you a little about myself in the hope that by understanding my background you will see what motivates me. You will see that I genuinely want both you and me to succeed beyond our wildest dreams.

My grandmother raised me on a small tobacco farm in Fairmont, North Carolina. We were relatively poor but never lacked the real necessities. My grandmother always had a garden, and we raised much of our own livestock. I went to work for neighboring farmers when I was six and worked in the tobacco fields practically every year until I graduated from high school. This was how I paid for my school clothes and supplies every year.

While growing up, I listened to my grandmother share her basic Christian values with my two younger brothers and me. We learned to be fair, honest, and self-sufficient. We learned to live by the golden rule and to treat others as we wanted to be treated.

We grew up poor—but happy. My mother and father separated when I was about four. My father took my two older brothers with him as he moved from one U.S. Army site to another. My grandmother took the three youngest boys so that my mother could move to the Northeast where wages were higher. She settled in Connecticut, but she didn't help the family she left behind on the farm. We found ourselves on welfare and struggling just to make a house payment.

I would only later realize what we missed growing up. Many people in my community did not know about the luxuries that people with more money enjoyed. Now that I am in the upper middle class, I choose to reflect—to appreciate how far I have come.

- *Our two-bedroom house never had air-conditioning and often lacked heat.*

- *I was 14 before I ever went to a movie theater.*

- *I was 16 before I ever tasted steak.*

- *When I turned 17, I got a part-time factory job and bought the first car my immediate family had ever owned.*

- *We did not have a telephone or television for most of my youth and teen years.*

- *Dental and medical treatment was only available when we were really sick. Preventive medicine didn't exist for us.*

- *The farmers I worked for misused pesticides and herbicides, exposing us to all kinds of poisons.*

Yet despite all of the hardships, life was pleasant. We had a lot of love and felt secure. My grandmother made one very important purchase while we were growing up, a set of World Book Encyclopedias. In my spare time, I went through practically every volume of that set. Reading those encyclopedias shaped my future and helped me to earn outstanding grades.

By the time I was a junior in high school, my teachers noticed my potential and steered me toward college. Only 10 percent of the students from my neck of the woods went to college, so I began preparing late. However, I applied and was accepted to three different universities. I went to the only one I had visited. It was near the annual state fair.

I attended North Carolina State University. It was a slight struggle in some classes because I had not taken all of the right preparatory classes. However, I persisted and eventually excelled. I watched other students, much smarter and much better prepared than I was, fail the college experience. I changed my major from biology to business and economics in my junior year because I planned to own my own business some day.

I also enrolled in Air Force ROTC in my junior year, and was commissioned as an officer in the U.S. Air Force upon graduation where I attended flight school to become a navigator. I was assigned to C-130 transport planes and got to see much of the world over the next two decades. My travels took me to Cuba, Puerto Rico, Panama, Honduras, the Bahamas, Bermuda, Grenada, Antigua, Dominica, England, Germany, France, Spain, Portugal, Greece, Italy, Turkey, the Philippines, Japan, Korea, Guam, Tinian, Saipan, Thailand, Vietnam, Laos, Cambodia, Singapore, Indonesia, and lots of other places that have faded into memory. In all of these places I felt that the people were approachable and really no different from me. I learned to love and respect all nationalities.

While in college, I discovered karate. It taught me discipline and self-assuredness. As I traveled from country to country in the military, I continued studying my beloved karate. Eventually, I introduced my daughters to karate, and they both rapidly earned their brown belts. I earned the coveted black belt. As I aged, karate became my method of maintaining fitness and tranquility.

Near the end of my military career, I decided to pursue my dream of owning my own business. It seemed natural to start something on the Internet since I was not sure where I would eventually settle down, and an Internet business was portable.

I spent hundreds of hours surfing the Internet, reading everything I could find. I also purchased several books and courses. I printed out hundreds of pages of articles. I subscribed to more than 100 Ezines. I read and I studied. Like most of you, I was looking for the secret to success in this business. I would eventually discover that there are no real secrets. It takes hard work, persistence, and a worthwhile product or service.

When I felt I was ready to take the plunge, I built several small Web sites. I built sites at Hypermart, Angelfire, and FreeYellow. I signed up for about 15 affiliate programs and loaded these sites down with banners and links. Then I sat back and waited for the orders to flood in. They didn't. I got a few orders every now and then but not many. During this same time I started a Web site mailing list to which I sent my Ezine. My subscriber list grew steadily.

Then one day I got an e-mail accusing me of being a fly-by-night company and asking why I didn't have my own domain name Web site. This told me two things: that people were interested in what I was selling and that they weren't sure they could trust me. After much soul searching, I took the plunge and decided to build a Web site using a professional host. I chose Virtualis and began building my Web site and Web presence. Business began to grow and I upgraded several times.

During all of my time online, I noticed that business grew fastest when I didn't really concentrate on selling but concentrated on trying to help others who were trying to start businesses. When I shared my experiences and advice freely with those who requested it, I received a lot of unexpected orders. This is perhaps the biggest key to my online success. I discovered that you have to give before you can receive. The things that I had been taught on my grand-

mother's knee turned out to be the things I needed to know for business success.

I am in business online to make a comfortable living. However, I genuinely want to see those who come to me seeking advice succeed also. I have struggled and succeeded. I want to help you to do the same.

A few of my Web sites and projects for you to check out when you have time follow below.

In 2003 I hosted my first workshop, which I called "The Internet Marketing How to Workshop." At this workshop we taught people how to create and market their own information products over the Internet. This is now an annual event that you can read about at *www.InternetMarketingHowToWorkshop.com.*

Since I learned to cook "country" foods while growing up on the farm, I've built a site around my "soul food." You can check out that site and even buy my cookbook at *www.Chitterlings.com.* After having a number of people ask me how I wrote my cookbook and how they could do the same, I put together a tele-class on the topic. It featured two other friends who had also written and self-published cookbooks. We recorded the whole thing and now offer the recording at *WriteACookbook.com.*

The biggest problem with many Web sites is that they simply don't make any sales; I sought and found the solution to that problem. The flaw was that the Web sites were often so poorly written that they didn't motivate anyone to make any purchases. I found a Web copywriting course that solves that problem and offer it at *PowerCopywritingForTheInternetByBobSerling.com.*

I also found a report on how to increase Web site conversions that allowed me to double my personal conversion rates. I bought the reprint rights to that course and now market it at *TheRealSe-*

*crets.com/thebook. As you can see, I have a lot of Web sites which would seem to be expensive but I spend less than $8 per year for registering each domain I own. I have my own domain name registration service, which I invite you to use. You can read all about it at **www.WillieCrawford.com/domains**.*

*I also spend very little for full-featured Web hosting. I use a company that charges me $25 per month for the first domain I host with them. Each additional domain (sharing the same Web space) costs me only $5 per month. This is how I can afford to have HUNDREDS of Web sites. You can check out my host at **www. WillieCrawford.com/myhost.html**.*

I have more projects going at any one time than you can shake a stick at. However, I do make time for my friends. I host a free weekly brainstorming session that you are welcome to join. It's on a first come, first serve basis and you'll need to pre-register. You can get full details on it call by sending an e-mail to my auto responder at willie3-56875@autocontactor.com. I also do one-on-one consulting for a handful of clients. You can get details on that at WillieCrawford.com/consultations.html.

The biographical sketch above is reprinted from Willie Crawford's "About Us" page.

Irena Whitfield

Name: Irena Whitfield
Web site: www.thecassiopeia.com

Irena Whitfield has been an entrepreneur for all her professional life, both offline and online, owning several companies and working in international business and finance for more than 15 years. During the past five years she specialized in Internet business consulting, became an author and lecturer, and now helps individuals and companies both offline and online to succeed in a highly competitive business environment.

As a computer systems engineer, she provides the right combination of services, especially for people striving to succeed in their home business on the Internet. On her Web site you can constantly receive up-to-date marketing and business tips, unique services, fast help, and Webmaster resources and tools necessary for an efficient and profitable online business.

Over the years in the business, she gained experience, skills, tricks, and routines on top of her technical background that make her help to 'netpreneurs so successful and effective. Foreign exchange trading and the years spent in business also gave her the discipline necessary for success in these fields.

Irena is the author of the bestselling eBooks, *7 Stars of Online Success, Success Tips and Tricks, The Success Seeds: the Entrepreneurial Bible* and other successful books, reports, and articles. She has contributed to *Women on Writing*, published by the National Association of Women Writers, and she is the owner of a quality online e-Publishing House with an excellent affiliate program paying 50 percent commissions to affiliates and Web Lions' Community and Library at **www.thecassiopeia.com/ ePublishing**.

She is also the Publisher of *"Pathway to Success,"* a successful FREE Ezine, sent to more than 138,000 subscribers every other Sunday that helps its readers succeed in their online home business by providing hot marketing tips, top Web master resources, business opportunities, articles, FREE Ads, Subscriber Corner, Web Lions' Library, and motivational reading.

- *Visitor Issue: **www.thecassiopeia.com/Portal/ Newsletter.html.***

- *Subscriber Issue: **www.thecassiopeia.com/WebLions/ Pathway.***

- *You can get special Gifts at **www.thecassiopeia.com/ WebLions/Pathway/SpecialGift2.html.***

Irena's Internet success story has taken several different directions and several years to achieve, as she tells us.

In fact, I have worked on the 'Net three times, every time in a completely different branch:

1. *In 1992: Program Transfer. I started when my business partner and I were developing computer programs and needed to test them with various partners in different countries. The Internet, though extremely slow at that time, was the answer for the program transfer.*

2. *In 1997: Forex trading. For five years I worked as a Forex trader and in 1997 started to use the Internet.*

3. *In 2000: Online home business started. For six years now, I have been active as an Internet Business Consultant. I started from scratch, personally researching, testing, and participating in everything I recommend to my clients and subscribers. I own the site: **www.thecassiopeia.com**.*

Her first product to be offered was found through of all sources, SPAM! It was SFI:

One day I received an e-mail from a SPAMmer offering a free SFI course. As I waited for my trades to close I signed up for the course and liked it so much that it inspired me to start my own online business. You can start too by clicking here: ***www.thecassiopeia.com/HomeBasedBusinessopportunity/SFI.html,*** ***www.thecassiopeia.com/HomeBasedBusinessopportunity/IAHBE.html.***

We asked her the most important characteristics for succeeding.

- ***Automatic traffic.*** *First I learned how to create customer and search-engine-friendly pages that get indexed fast, ranked at the top and receiving automatic and targeted traffic. Once I knew how to do this, I created my overall long-term project. This was around May-June 2000.*

- ***Overall project of my business.*** *The tool was my Web site. I decided on the industry field, theme, layout, colors, logos, names, and everything else necessary for the site. Then I decided that the core of the project would be a free online course which I developed. The project also contained a free Ezine and my books. When I finished the project in my head, I simply created it and launched it all at once in September 2000. Within the first 14 days my site was indexed and ranked number one on all the biggest search engines and on hundreds of small search engines for the basic keyword phrases, and still is! Now it's top ranked for hundreds of keyword phrases.*

- ***Content Web site.*** *Since the very beginning I knew it would be a large and free content site. So, I built it. Now it has more than 18,000 pages and links, and I continue to add new pages and sections almost every day. It's fun, I love my work and it's very profitable! Check out* ***www.thecassiopeia.com.***

- ***"Pathway to Success" Ezine.*** *I knew I wouldn't be willing to pay for traffic or advertising and I knew I needed to be in contact with my audience regularly, so it was clear I had to have an Ezine. When I launched the first issue in December 2000,* *it had one subscriber. Today "Pathway to Success" is published to more than 138,500 registered subscribers, and thousands of people receive it using my automatic publishing tools. Basically new subscriptions are very limited now, and I am thinking of stopping these altogether. It's at **www.thecassiopeia.com/ WebLions/Pathway**.*

- *Books. My books were part of the original project but implemented later. From time to time I add new books and reports. The majority of the books are for sale but tons of the others are free. You can get them within the Web Lions' Library, "Pathway to Success" Archives and ePublishing at **www. thecassiopeia.com/ePublishing.***

I would stress that it is absolutely necessary to know exactly what you want to do—what you want to achieve and why. The next step is to create or find the tools you need to make your work effective and efficient to reach success in the fastest and easiest way. Jumping from one program or idea to another just doesn't lead anywhere. I can tell you that I still stick to my first overall project and definitely the long-term goal.

Of course, you need discipline, persistence, and enthusiasm. You must be willing to learn, improve, make qualified decisions, take calculated risks, work properly, and act in order to succeed.

Don't believe in any hype, overnight miracles, get-rich-quick-schemes and the like. The only person able to make miracles is you through the work you put into your business.

Wishing you all the best in everything you do and remember: "If one doesn't know to which port one is sailing, no wind is favorable."

— Seneca

Kevin Bidwell

Name: Kevin Bidwell

Address: 956 South Highway 25W • Williamsburg, KY 40769

Phone: 423-784-6300

Kevin Bidwell has been called "The Web Marketing Wizard" and "one of the best copywriters on the Web." Since 1988 he has been helping ordinary people achieve extraordinary results in business and in life. Through his consulting, writing, and speaking he has worked with thousands of business people to develop the plans, find the resources, and secure the products to make their business a success. Since 1988 he has spoken to audiences of more than 200,000 people, teaching them to use the same insider tactics that he uses to make his own businesses successful.

His own sites receive more than 300,000 hits per month, and **All-In-One-Business.com** is ranked by **Alexa.com** as one of the top .01 percent (yes, that's 1/10 of 1 percent) of all Web sites, and by Trafficranking.com as one of the top 10 "get into business" Web sites. Kevin teaches his clients to do the same—on a shoestring budget.

He lives on a farm in Williamsburg, Kentucky, in the middle of Appalachian culture.

> *Because of my wife's illness in 2000 I realized I needed to be home with my family more. In October of that year, I purchased Cory Rudl's course and then went online in January 2001. My first product was actually a lead-generating, free e-mail course. I later adapted that into the original Success Secrets course.*

The elements of success for Kevin stemmed from his great inner beliefs.

From the beginning I have always known I would succeed. Knowing deep inside that success will eventually come imparts perseverance through all of the setbacks. It allowed me to lose—more than once—and still be positive and productive in my work.

*Know that you can succeed online. If you are using a good resource as a guide (I have a list of them on my Web site at **www.All-In-One-Business.com**), you can succeed. Will it be easy? No. Nothing worthwhile ever is. Keep plugging away and you will be successful. It's not random. It's not chance. A solid plan coupled with perseverance will bring online success.*

Kevin Nunley

Name: Kevin Nunley
Phone: 603-249-9519
E-mail: kevin@drnunley.com

Before starting his own business on the Internet, Kevin Nunley spent 21 years working in management and on the air at major television and radio stations. During that time he obtained an insider view of how the media can be used to promote the success of people and organizations.

Kevin has written many books, articles, and courses. He now writes articles for Ezines and marketing publications. Having an insider's view of media, he offers great marketing advice and copy writing and promotional tools that teach people how to succeed by knowing how to use the media wisely.

He advises against using traditional business tactics on the Internet and stresses adjusting marketing strategies specifically for 'Net use. He makes no promises of riches overnight and is very straightforward about hard work, creativity, and dedication.

Because many of Kevin's articles are printed on AOL, in popular business magazines, and on Prodigy, he tends to get many high recommendations and is well respected in the industry.

He has more than 10,000 marketing tips for you to peruse free of charge. See his site at **DrNunley.com**. Or you can reach him at kevin@drnunley.com or even telephone him at 603-249-9519.

What has made him so successful?

- He used his valuable experience within the media to write many articles and informational books to help businesses promote their products and services.

- He used his talents as a writer to build his business through his articles.

- He filled a large growing need for information on business promotion.

Kevin provided the following articles when asked about his advice for beginning entrepreneurs.

Successful Service Selling By Kevin Nunley©

To sell your product or service successfully, set your goal to win clients, not assignments. Your income will grow larger if you have regular clients who keep coming back. Go out of your way to please your clients and do a good job for them. No matter how busy or successful you are, it is important to come across as someone who is helpful, not someone who is "snobby."

There have been more than a few cases where we had to bend over backward for a difficult client. Later those customers went on to recommend us to many others, obviously impressed that we made the effort to please them.

Build personal relationships with as many people as you can—even people who you might consider unimportant could someday have a major say over whether you are hired. Try to participate in client activities. Make sure that you say hello to your clients at conferences and other events in your industry.

Remember, clients have power. Never be rude or lose your temper. Always try to be patient, courteous, and friendly. Clients can choose not to continue working with you at any time, for any reason, or sometimes for no reason at all.

How to Build Your Money-Making E-mail List

By Kevin Nunley©

Kevin started his e-mail list in 1996 and sends his subscribers information like this every week. Subscribe and see his hundreds of helpful business articles at drnunley.com.

I'm often asked, "What's the best way to build a business when you don't have much money to spend?" I never hesitate when I answer. Build your own e-mail list!

A good e-mail list that YOU COLLECTED YOURSELF is worth its weight in gold. My list that I started with an AOL account and pasting subscriber addresses into Text Pad now generates six figures in sales every year. I know a consultant who pulls down even more with her home-grown e-mail list. And there's the guy who keeps his business humming by sending his thoughts to his list whenever he feels like it, once a month, once every three months, or once a week.

None of these people has any special tricks to use a list to generate $17,000 in a weekend. You've probably seen sales pitches that promise that. They simply attract people who are interested in getting their information, put them on their list, and send them *good info on a regular basis.*

If subscribers don't buy from you now, they will eventually. It's standard to hear from new customers, "I've been getting your newsletter for years and figured it was time to buy."

Your e-mail list becomes a running source of non-stop sales for you. Want to know how most of the successful online businesses stay profitable year after year? They have a good list. Want to know why so many small businesses fold within months of starting? They don't have a list. It's often as simple as that.

How do you get your list? Here are several commonly used ways. The original and most common method to get people to subscribe to your list is to offer information. Offer a newsletter filled with information of real value to a specific audience. Offer free reports, white papers, or e-mail alerts. When people buy from you, get their e-mail addresses. Have your order form ask if it's all right to send them valuable information from time to time. Usually more than half will say yes.

Create a contest and have people subscribe to your newsletter as a requirement for entry. Of course, you will give them a chance to unsubscribe after the contest is over, but most will opt to keep receiving your messages.

Now, let me get all gloomy and say a few words about purchasing lists of names. Lists of addresses you buy, even from the best of sources, usually don't work very well. For some reason the immense power of an e-mail list doesn't kick in until people learn about you and THEN sign up to get your information. It doesn't work very well to send information to people who have never heard of you. You can send and send until you're blue in the face, but few will ever buy anything.

OK, all that sounds good. But where do you get the information to send to your list? "Kevin, you're a WRITER. This stuff is easy for you, but I HATE to write!" I can hear you cry. And that's exactly the reason you should use my articles or the articles of any other writer who will allow you to use them, and most will if you also include their contact information at the end of the article.

Subscribe to lists that cover the same information you do. When you see a great article, e-mail the author and ask for permission to reprint it. You can also paraphrase information you find. Just put the information in your own words.

List-building is highly effective, but it's not a get-rich-quick method. It often takes a full year to get your list up to the point where it starts getting results for you. It could take several years before it becomes a source of income that seriously changes your lifestyle, but in the scope of things, that's a pretty quick way to achieve the success you deserve.

Michael T. Glaspie

In case you have not heard of "Mike G," as he is commonly called, here is a short introduction: Michael T. Glaspie is the chairman and founder of Webnet International, one of the nation's largest privately held Internet service companies. He started Webnet International as the foundational organization for the development of independent, yet synergistic, Internet companies covering the gamut of advertising resources commonly used for effective, targeted Web advertising.

He is also the creator of Spam Terminator™, a downloadable desktop utility. It is the first universally applicable and effective SPAM blocking software developed. It was designed to be marketed both online and offline as it can be installed as an ISP application at the PC construction level for manufacturers and sold through retail distribution. International licensing and ISP inquiries are invited.

Webnet International serves as the parent company to these now widely recognized membership-based Web services with a combined membership and subscriber database of nearly 1.5 million. All of these sites are well within the top 1 percent of all Web sites visited on the Web.

- BannersGoMLM.com, **www.bannersgomlm.com** – Offers you free Unlimited Advertising for Life – and a $15 Signing Bonus. It is the world's fastest growing advertising exchange and the only free MLM program that's legal everywhere in the world. No cost. No risk. No downside. It automatically markets itself from your site and Serves approximately 200 million banners per month.

- BannerCo-op.com, **www.bannerco-op.com** – The first and only advertising co-op featuring a 1:1 exchange on all earned impressions plus cash for clicks on banners on member's sites. It serves about 50 million banners per month.

- FreeLinks'Network.com, **www.freelinksnetwork.com** – A powerful free traffic generating tool for Webmasters in all industries.

- FreeMarketingInfo.business at **www.freemarketinginfo. business** and CDFREE.TV, **www.cdfree.TV** – These two sites offer Mr. Glaspie's 68-minute tutorial seminar instructing 'netpreneurs on effective Web site construction, strategies, and marketing methods.

Having previously built a telecommunications organization from scratch to an $18 million plus per annum success story, Michael now devotes himself to helping others "figure it out" by teaching hopeful 'netpreneurs how to market any product, service, program or opportunity on the net.

Michael's direct marketing career has spanned two decades and includes authorship of four books and three home study courses, including more than 50 hours of audio cassette instructional material and 20 hours of live "marketing through technology" boot camp video recordings. These $5,500-per-seat "Marketing through Technology" boot camps have sold out at each scheduled conference.

His works, all dealing with the common theme "Marketing through Technology" include:

- *Hot Wires - Secrets of the 900-Number Industry*
- *"1-900"-Opportunity*
- *Unleash the Entrepreneur Within*
- *The Ultimate Money Machine*
- *Profits Online*
- *'Net Marketing 2005*

Michael has also served in public office as an elected trustee for two terms in his home community. He has served as president of the Michigan Rental Housing Association where he has frequently met with legislators in successful efforts to write and pass laws affecting rental housing and practices.

He shared his keys to success with us.

I am always interested in helping people learn about marketing. Direct marketing is just a way to distribute services and infor-mation. So many people are beating their heads against a wall, and it doesn't have to be that way. It is just a learning curve that everyone needs to go through to achieve his or her goals. It is very possible for people to achieve their goals online.

Regarding my first Internet business, up until 1997 I owned a fairly successful long-distance telephone company. In fact, we owned our own tariffs and we could charge whatever we liked. We had offices in all 50 states and 70,000 independent representatives selling our long distance service around the county. We were the first company to offer prepaid custom phone cards. It's an interesting story.

Part of the business that we owned consisted of pay phones. I spent a lot of money setting up these pay phones. In Florida alone, we had them in all the major ports where I had a ton of money tied up in them. Pay phones at ports and terminals typically get a huge amount of volume. They were sitting in Florida for eight weeks, and I kept checking the reports, but those phones simply were not making any money. I said to myself, "This is just not right." So I got on a plane and flew into Orlando and went to Port Canaveral, to try to figure out what was wrong with my pay phones—all beautiful phones set on a pedestal with a roof on top, first-rate, first-class all the way. I went up to the pedestals and walked all around. People would get off the ships, especially the ships' employees, and they all wanted to call someone.

I looked down and noticed the ground was littered with small pieces of paper—disposable phone cards. You buy one for about $2, make calls with the access number on the back, and then throw it away. People were using prepaid phone cards to make their long distance calls on my pay phones, but I wasn't making any money! In fact I was losing money.

As a result, three months later we were the first company to come out with rechargeable, custom, prepaid phone cards in the United

States Today many of our cards are collectible items. We were commissioned to do a prepaid phone card for the Papal visit to the United States in 1993. That was a huge success for the organizations that distributed the cards for us.

We did a number of custom, prepaid phone cards like this. We did the artwork in-house. It looked like a credit card and you never had to throw it away. The card had two toll-free numbers on the back. Obviously, one was used to make the phone call and the other one was for—you guessed it—putting more money on the card.

*I started this successful business from scratch in 1991 and sold it around 1996. This is when I landed in the Internet business. When I sold the card company, I kept a few people on, and we sat down and said, "Let's figure out the Internet." We had no idea what we were doing, but we knew the Internet had a huge potential as the next "thing" and we wanted to do something with it. We proceeded to develop our first product, **www.mysite.com**, a way to give away free Web sites, but it hasn't been updated in quite a while.*

Back then, because businesses were not connected to the Internet, the marketplace was offline. We developed a brochure reminiscent of the yellow pages. On the cover was written, "Just like the yellow pages, your business needs a Web site." We distributed these by the truckload! People would get it in the mail and read about all the things their free Web site would give them. We let them send us all the info about their business. They could even fax their sales pages! Many customers chose the basic Web site which we set up absolutely free, but we also offered many options in a kit with monthly fees. These things were not common then as they are now. The average ticket came to about $22 a month.

As the business ran its course, we had 77,000 monthly paying customers. That was our first venture. We had a product for use on the World Wide Web, but we marketed it offline. The market-

place is still enormous for selling offline. If you can find a way to market online, you can find a way to sell offline!

I knew we were onto something big because I attended a conference when we were putting all this together. I sent off a check for some ad copy to the USA Today *newspaper. While we were at the conference, I received a phone call from my office saying that the editor had rejected the ad. I left the conference and called them on my cell phone. I asked, "What's up? You won't accept my ad? My check is good! What is the deal?" They said, "We are not going to run the ad because we regard the Web as a competing media."*

Right then I knew I was onto something big. If a major newspaper regarded my little business as competition, hey baby, let me have at it! Of course that is no longer the case. I knew then that all newspapers would have their own Web sites, and they would also offer advertising to their clients. An enormous amount of revenue can be made by offering various advertising on Web sites. All of that changed after a short period of time, but I was the first person ever to place an ad in a major publication worth a couple of thousand dollars, and they turned me down because they thought I was competition. I knew we had a winner! That was our first venture, and since then we have gone on to do so many wonderful things on the Internet!

It is not uncommon for folks to request my time to help them accomplish their goals on the Internet. I always do the absolute best I can to help people who come to me to help them in their business. You don't know this, but I give away more free stuff than any other marketer.

Banner advertising is big business! Banners took a bashing because many advertising companies wanted to prove that banners don't work because they wanted advertisers to try some other form of advertising. But look at the stats: $1.3 billion can't be wrong.

I can tell you what motivated me, but different people have different motivations. Some want the freedom to do what they want, financial freedom, or to set flexible hours with the freedom to work at home. Obviously the objective is to make more money and enjoy the freedom of just having your own business. For me it has always been a matter of selling. I actually sold pens, pencils, and erasers from my desk when I was in third grade, and the teachers let me get away with it. When I was 15 years old I bought a pickup truck and paid cash for it when I could not even drive! But that did not stop me. This is the American way. I hired my brother to drive it and started my own lawn care service with all my buddies. I paid my help $1 per hour and charged my clients $2 per hour. My brother drove the truck, dropped everyone off in the morning and picked them up in the evening.

Everyone has specific reasons for starting a business but the main thing is to set it up right in the beginning and to do it properly. You can set up a corporation and take advantage of starting up your own business under a corporate umbrella. There are many things people need to learn, and anything we have talked about you can look up in the search engines. You need to have a business with value that you can sell, not some "mom and pop" business that does not have much value and when you are gone, it is gone too. Many people start a business without any products. They just join affiliate programs and sell to their lists. That is another way of building your business. Lists are very important in any company.

As with any undertaking, there are obstacles. Michael's story is no different.

My biggest obstacle was overcoming the technical learning curve. We have a number of programmers who work with us. Without a basic understanding of how things work and function I would be at the mercy of these people to design my Web sites and structure my businesses.

*If you let someone else decide what is going to be done, that person is going to do it from a technical point of view, not a sales point of view. Everything needs to be carefully orchestrated. I have a great course called "Seize Your Marketing Potential No Sales Pitch from Nine Top Marketers" at **www.nobsmarketinghelp.com**—16 hours of hard, solid learning for $1 down. I do not make any money on the course. It is there for your readers to study and enjoy.*

To what does he attribute his success?

- *My ability to think creatively, to look at a product and service, and see how it can be presented differently or combined with another offer so that it can become a whole new product or service.*

- *My ability to take punches from critics. You have to be able to take the criticism, learn from it, or forget about being in business.*

- *My determination to excel. Anyone who wants to be successful learns from their mistakes and is determined to succeed.*

- *Have no fear! Find someone to joint venture with and let rejection roll off your back.*

- *One of the most wonderful traits among successful people is that they are interested in sharing with others. Early on, I would seek out those who were tops in their field, and through them I learned and grew. Seek advice and then follow it. Do not keep pestering a mentor. Take the advice and move forward.*

*My highest success is yet to come! I am building **www.Zabang. com**. It has two slogans: "I got Zabang at Zabang.com" and "It's fast, relevant and people love it." I have put an enormous amount of energy into this business for about a year to create the best search engine ever. Is this going to be competition for Google and other search engines? Google? Well, those guys are going to be hard to topple, but we are doing things at Zabang that no one else has considered. For instance, our promise is to build Zabang from the net up, not from corporate down. We already have 31,844 pre-registered affiliates for that site and more to come. They will have our search bar on their Web site and it is amazing. We are going to pay our affiliates 10 percent on the first level. No, this is not Internet marketing. This is a two-tier affiliate program. When an affiliate sends traffic to Zabang.com, the affiliate will get 10 percent of any advertising, packages, or anything else that the customer ever purchases through Zabang solutions. It is the site where people will go to purchase pay-per-click advertising, and affiliates will earn 10 percent for the life from that customer in exchange for sending the customer one time to Zabang.*

Is this similar to Adsense? An interesting comment on the famous Google Adsense: Google made some mistakes with this. They made it incentive based. Major advertisers, and I am one, are very disgruntled with the way ads on sites are subject to click frauds.

Zabang will never do this. Zabang will not in any way be incentive-based. We are paying out 5 percent on second level. It is going to be unique. For example, when you type your keyword, our third result down will say, "Congratulations. Zabang has found a coupon that we think is relevant to your search keyword entered." We have done this by partnering up with two of the largest coupon venders on the net. From their RSS feed (Really Simple Syndication or Rich Site Summary) we instantly receive notification when the search word is entered, and then we apply our own algorithm. It is all about productivity: thinking outside the box. Ask yourself what other products and services you can add to your current products that will make you totally unique in the market? We are doing a number of things like this at Zabang that we think will make people use Zabang search engine. Hopefully they'll say, "I should check Zabang and see if there are any money-saving coupons." That is just one of the reasons that we think we will have repeat customers—because we have a unique service.

We have already signed a contract with a major university. This contract will give us every imaginable paper ever written for any search term you enter having to do with medical or science topics, absolutely free. For example, if you type in "Cardiac Arrest" you will get the message, "Congratulations. Zabang has found for you a white paper on Cardiac Arrest" and you get the download right then. You do not have to go to any other Web site. We are doing a lot of things like this, all of them consumer-oriented, that will make people say, "I need to check out Zabang."

I can hear people who are reading this saying, "You will never be able to compete with Google, MSN, and Yahoo!," but they are wrong. I have gone up against ATT, right? And you can do these things. Your only obstacle is convincing the consumer that they should be using your service and getting them to return on a regular basis.

Zabang is really going to be a place people will to want to see with our enormous network of affiliates who are most anxious to carry our search bar on their Web site (and the present count of 30,000 is just a drop in the bucket compared with what it is going to be).

You may ask, how are you going to sell advertising when you are competing against Google and MSN? Well, I have a surprise for you! If you buy keyword advertising, you are always on the lookout for new places to advertise and buy more advertising. It is not a budget issue. If you have a campaign and you know that every time your keyword gets clicked on you make a profit, you want to place ads for that same keyword, right? Advertisers can place that same ad for that same keyword, right? Recognize that the Internet is all about direct response. Advertisers on the Internet are not interested in branding. They simply say, "Here is our slogan. Click here to buy now."

There is an endless, bottomless pool of advertising resources. Our only objective now is to build a Web site that people enjoy and want to use. That is why we are loading up Zabang.com with very consumer-oriented benefits just for having them use it. We want people to check it out.

What about failures?

I have had a couple. I won't mention the Web site names but I take full responsibility for their failures because I depended on someone else to do things that they did not do, and I lost track of it. I have learned some lessons. Here's lesson number one—focus. If you are in the mode of building your business, stay on it, stay focused, no matter who else is involved until it is at a point when you can let go of the reins. Don't turn your back on it and go onto the next project thinking all is well because if you do, you are setting yourself up for failure.

Who has most influenced him in his business success?

There have been many mentors over the years but one man in particular stands out. His name was Lewis J. Seaton. I met the late Mr. Seaton when I was a young man. I worked for him for several weeks tending to chores around his mansion. At that time he was vice president of personnel for General Motors and was the man who negotiated with the head of the United Auto Workers (UAW). It was his job to protect the company coffers when writing contracts with the UAW, and he held that role for about 20 years. He was a marvelous, marvelous man. I came from an underprivileged background, and I went to work for him during the summer. I remember one time he tossed me the keys to his Cadillac Eldorado. I remember it had a car phone in it, quite unheard of in 1966, and he said, "Mike, I want you to run down to the hardware store for me." I told him I would be happy to take my own car but he said, "No, Mike, I am serious about this. I want you to learn how the other half lives." What he taught me is that there is a whole other world out there. You just have to open your eyes to see it. You can be that other half. You just need to learn how to do it.

Let me share with you a few snippets of advice that I think, considered together, add up to a great packet of information.

- *Never give up. Stick with it until it succeeds or know when to walk away from it.*

- *Do exactly what you say you will do and then a little extra.*

- *Never, ever lose your temper or express yourself by phone or e-mail in a way that you will regret later. Get it out of your system before you reply.*

- *Don't devote your life to business. Business is just something you do. Everything else is your life.*

I do not have a favorite publication, but I am an avid reader. I read a minimum of one new business book every month. I also subscribe to a number of Ezines and read them daily. I'm familiar with most of the things going on in the market today, but I read them looking for those little nuggets—maybe something I forgot about or something that's new. By following the advice of well-known authors with credentials, you can literally become a PhD of Marketing on the 'Net in just a few months. Devour everything you can get your hands on. You can find so much free material on the Internet that it is just mind-boggling.

Michael's advice for budding entrepreneurs today:

Find something you would like to spend your time doing even if you were never paid a dime for it. Assume that you already have all the money in the world, and this one thing is what you would like to do for the rest of your life. What is your hot button? There is no hobby, endeavor, or field of interest where people are not getting rich at it in some way. Not one. Whatever your interest is, there is a way to make money with it in some way, some place, somehow, or through a related endeavor connected with that field of interest. Find it! This is introspective time. Get away from your responsibilities and go somewhere to think. Decide what you like the most and then do it. People are making money by following this philosophy. You can have your own product or you can be an affiliate in the field. Start by searching for your area of interest online; then set up a homepage for it, optimize the keywords for robot crawls, and begin your business.

*Never use a free domain name. Always buy a top-level domain name (.com, .net, or .org – preferably .com) because you cannot get indexed at any of the major search engines with a free sub-domain (for example, **www.mybusiness.tripod.com**) and it looks very unprofessional. People always say to me, "I have been promoting this program for six months now. I've submitted it to all the search engines but I am not getting anywhere." Then I look up the URL only to find a sub-domain. That is the reason they haven't been successful. You've got to have your own top level domain with a great Web page, and the world opens up for you, even if you are just copying an affiliate mirror page, because then you have your own page to advertise. Offer your visitors an Ezine and/or free report unique to your site, and then you can start building the second* *most important thing in business—YOUR OWN database.*

To recap: *Find what you like doing, set up your own Web site, and advertise. Participate in joint ventures and linking. All kinds of things can happen. If you do not know how to use keywords, research "search engine optimization." All sorts of free information can be found on the 'Net, or you can hire professionals to optimize your site for you. It comes down to just one thing. What would you do for the rest of your life if you had all the money in the world? The moment you answer that question, the rest of it is mechanical.*

You could always obtain my free CD for more information. I have also written many books. My first book was a sales letter bound into the book for my course. It is now a collector's item. It was titled, Hot Wires—The Secrets of the Exploding 900 Business. *I was in the 900 telephone number business before I started my own phone company. This was before it was ruined by unscrupulous businesses. I was the second person to take out a 900 number directly from ATT. I wrote a book about this emerging industry, and the last chapter of that book sold my study course for $225. The people who read the book bought the course. I have seen the book for sale for as much as $600 on eBay. I have a case of them unopened and am waiting for the price to go way up and then sell autographed copies of them. (Big smile.)*

Michael's advice for the rest of us?

Write good copy! Without a shadow of a doubt, once you have this skill:

- *All of the other mechanical pieces fall into place.*

- *Other marketers will recognize you and will want to be*

partners.

- *People who visit your site will want to do business with you.*

- *You will be able to prepare effective short copy for classified ads.*

- *You will be able to turn your attention to other ventures and businesses.*

- *You will be able to entice that reader to do business with you and buy your products.*

*I have posted a one-hour tutorial on effective sales letter copywriting. The material's format will cause you to slap yourself on the forehead and say, "Why didn't I think of that?" I have a little homework assignment for you. When you listen to this recording, it will make you laugh. But after you do this homework assignment, it will bring home to you just how easy this process is. It is free at **www.bannersgomlm.com/cgi-in/dl/nobsdl. cgi?Refid=salesletter.***

What legacy does he want to leave?

Just starting out in the world of business after college my thoughts were, "How am I going to provide for this new family of mine?" and "What am I going to achieve to make me a head taller than my competitors?" I didn't consider my legacy then. But now that I consider it, I want to leave behind a body of work that people can point to some day and say, "Here are the things that Mike G did that made life somehow a little better and a little more prosperous for everyone he touched."

Jan Tallent-Dandridge

Jan Tallent-Dandridge is the Marketing Warrioress at **www. jantd.com** and Publisher of Rim Digest Ezine, **www.rimdigest. com**. She tells her story:

I first tried out Internet marketing in December 1998. I loved the 'Net and wanted to see if someone really could make the money they were talking about at that time. I joined a couple of safe lists back when they were the rave and watched for a while to see what was "hot." I joined a reseller program that is no longer going, and as I started joining more and more affiliate programs I dropped the dead weight and stuck with those that at least paid their way.

My success, if it can be called that, was an accident. One of my upline members asked me to take over the Ezine she had taken over from another editor temporarily. I did not even want to do it. I knew I had no talent or knack for doing a newsletter, but as a favor to her I tried it. At the time I was getting almost 100 Ezines myself and knew what I liked and did not like so a little at a time I made teeny changes to the format of the Ezine I had taken over. People seemed to like ME. I was really shocked. The more ME I put in the Ezine, the more they forwarded it to friends, and the database went from 36 people in February of 1999 to 1000 in just three or four months. I was in awe!

I have had up to 70,000 so-called subs either by people subscribing—which is the only way I would do it now—or by buying out smaller Ezines and making an announcement and then adding them to my database, or by buying leads, which I learned the hard way is not for Ezine success, or at least, not for me.

I have been told it is my personal touch that has kept my subscribers. I do not believe in hype or exaggeration, and my credibility has been and remains the most important part of my life and my success.

My advice to someone starting out today is to be careful. As they say, if it seems too good to be true it is almost certainly a scam. Do not SPAM no matter what some expert might be recommending, and just be yourself. It goes a long way when all else might fail.

Tony Marino, PhD Marketing

Dr. Tony Marino is not only the CEO of "America Web Works" **www.AmericaWebWorks.com**, he is also host of the PodCast Radio Show radio.Weblogs.com/0144135, the founder of the **www.AudioVideoStreams.com**, the International ePublisher's Association, *Christian Times eBusiness Newsletter* and the author of the ePublishing Master's Course at **www.ePublisherUniversity.com**. He holds E-mail Compliance Officer status for many of today's leading network marketing companies.

He has also worked with the likes of legendary direct marketers Ted Nicholas and Gary Halbert; best-selling authors, Harvey McKay, Jack Canfield, and Mark Victor Hansen; ABC Television's Jimmy Kimmel, and NBC's Carson Daly, and online marketers, Dale Calvert and Jay Abraham, just to name a few. His offices are located in Portland and Los Angeles, and he'd love to hear from you anytime at **www.AmericaWebWorks.com** 866-824-9684.

This is Tony's success story.

> *Before coming online I worked extensively with TV and radio, Fox and NBC to name just two. I applied my experience and expertise to my first online business, American Web Works. It has grown into a large publishing, consulting, and marketing company. We currently publish eight newsletters and have helped countless clients market their businesses and develop successful enterprises.*
>
> *We saw opportunities on the Internet early and started "American*

Web Works" with a single newsletter in 1996, The Christian News Online. *At first it was a newsletter about Christian and religious topics, but after about two years our subscribers dictated a change. They asked me to introduce marketing tips and advice into the newsletter.* The Christian News Online *became the* Christian Marketer. *Our publications are all subscriber-oriented. We pay very close attention to our subscribers and have built our newsletters around them. Today we have eight newsletters and a large marketing consulting firm.*

What are the keys to his success?

- *Listening to subscribers and giving outstanding customer service.*

- *Dedication.*

- *Keeping an open mind.*

- *It is all about how you serve your audience.*

- *Take care of your customers and subscribers. Give great customer service and support.*

- *Treat everyone you come into contact with respect.*

- *Persevere.*

- *Do your research, keep up with trends, and keep abreast of the latest news in your field.*

- *Study carefully.*

- *Keep up with all e-mails and answer promptly – something that is often forgotten by businesses when they become successful.*

- *Always allow yourself to be available for comments, questions, or help.*

- *Do not ever mislead the public. Be honest. Viral marketing and good news about your business travels fast but negative news travels faster.*

His advice to beginning 'netpreneurs:

Never try to go it alone. Meet others. You can subscribe to newsletters and go to business forums and business networks, just to name a few places, where you can meet fellow business associates. Find a mentor who has been successful. Do your due diligence and research before you sign on with any mentoring or coaching service. Find someone who has been successful and give them a call.

Have a good reason to go into business—it should not be money. Have any other reason but do not go into business simply because you want to get rich. There is no such thing as getting rich quickly in business. Everything in business requires work and perseverance so you must truly have a motivating reason to be in business and want to succeed.

- *Think logically and plan carefully before making any decisions for your business.*

- *Research and keep ahead of the trends in marketing; always be knowledgeable and informed about your business topic.*

- *Decide on your business concept (USP).*

- *Hire experts whenever you need them. Nobody knows everything.*

- *Make sure any consulting firm you hire knows what they are doing and is there for you. Take time to build a relationship with them so that your efforts are coordinated and you are both on the same page.*

Tony's company is unique in its coaching methods. He and his associates take time to build a relationship with a client even before the contract is signed and the deal closed. This is one of the biggest keys to his success. Tony's Christian background and strong beliefs have influenced his entire business concept. The customer or subscriber is always first and is treated with respect and dignity.

Terry Dean

Terry Dean is a nine-year veteran of Internet marketing and author of numerous articles and books on marketing and making money online. He is a highly successful marketing coach and owns the coaching membership site **www.netbreakthroughs.com**.

Terry originally wanted to study theology and had no intention of starting a business but did a radical turn in 1996. At one point he was in considerable debt but now is enjoying the fruits of his hard-earned labor as a highly successful coach. He currently runs a worldwide company, Business Systems 2000, out of his home office in Indiana. He has helped many people because he takes on a diversified group in his market, allowing him to expand rapidly. He has written eBooks and produced audio and videotapes in his training material.

He now earns well into six figures a year while living what he likes to call the "Internet Lifestyle" (working only 20 to 30 hours a week). He understands the meaning of working for a goal and putting in 60 hours a week when he began. His was a two-person operation, only himself and his wife, but now his entire business runs almost completely on autopilot, leaving him time to spend with his family.

He has learned from the masters like Jay Abraham and continues to keep up with marketing trends, applying his knowledge to his service to bring his clients success. He is very people oriented, likes to build relationships with his clients, especially learning about their success in business—very beneficial for sales when he advertises to them.

His greatest asset is his well-targeted opt-in list for his newsletter. Terry was profitable in business in just under three months from the day he first bought his computer and went online. He really started to make money when he built his own opt-in list with his newsletter. He has a successful membership site, 'NetBreakthroughs, that shows his members exactly how to make money quickly and easily online.

How did he become successful?

- He became an expert in his field by educating himself.

- He used his people skills to create his coaching course.

- He saw a need for mentors in the business world, and he filled it.

- He was prepared to work hard to achieve his goals.

- He did not give up, no matter how difficult things became.

- He developed multiple incomes for his business.

- He built a newsletter and opt-in list.

- He automated his business and can now enjoy time with his wife and family.

Education is a very important part of starting and developing a successful business. Terry made sure he learned from the masters in the industry and continues to do so. He teaches his students to do the same.

- He made use of his teaching and people skills to create a coaching course and run a highly successful membership site where he can teach and coach many people at once, saving himself a lot of time.

- He recognized the need of startup businesses for people who could provide proper guidance. He filled that need at a reasonable cost that even a new business person could afford. He priced his product for his market.

- He was prepared to put in long hours to start and develop his business. Any startup business needs devotion, and Terry was not afraid to put in the necessary hours he needed to succeed.

- He was at one time in serious debt, but he did not let that stop him. He was determined to succeed.

- He developed multiple streams of income for his business: a membership coaching site, eBooks, and individual coaching, to name a few.

- He has made money from his newsletter, which has over 36,000 opt-in subscribers. When done correctly, this can be lucrative.

- He has automated many of the tasks in his business,

allowing him more time to relax and develop new streams of income.

Bill Platt

Name: Bill Platt

Location: Enid, Oklahoma USA

Phone: 580-242-3367

Web site: www.ThePhantomWriters.com

I started my first online business in 1997. It was not well thought-out and turned into a prime flop.

I launched my second online business in 1999. This time, I focused on a product I knew something about, but beyond the newsletter I had little hope for success. I built it without giving much thought as to how I would generate cash for my efforts. I had an early concept, but it was a tough sell in a saturated market. Within the first six months I had a well-respected newsletter, but I did not earn an income from it.

*When you are ready to drive traffic to your Web site, you need to create educational materials on a subject that you know. By educating rather than selling, you will find that more publishers and Webmasters will be inclined to share your knowledge with their readers and visitors and they will do it for free. When you have your materials together, let me help you reach the publishers and Webmasters who seek your knowledge and insight. If you need help to find your voice, I can assist with that as well at **ThePhantomWriters.com**.*

*I started my third online business in 2000, it was transformed into **ThePhantomWriters.com**. I have made money every month since—some months earning boatloads of money. This business* *model has kept me at home with my children full-time during most of last year. As for the first product, it was a free-reprint article I wrote and submitted to **InternetDay.com**, circa 1999. This project turned my career from that of writing an Ezine to writing articles for the general Internet public. The first service that I sold in the open market was ghostwriting articles for other busy online business owners.*

What personal characteristics were necessary for success?

- *Above all else – persistence – not quitting when the job was tough, sticking to the plan while I worked outside my home – I worked 60 hours a week on the job and 25 to 30 hours a week building the foundations of my home business.*

- *Second, confidence – believing in myself when no one around me thought I'd succeed.*

- *Next, a strong work ethic; 85 to 100 hours a week is a real commitment to any task. I kept myself on that schedule, even when I was wiped out and too tired to think, sending out just one more alliance-building e-mail before the day was done.*

- *Building alliances with clients, acquaintances, and sometimes competitors.*

In a nutshell, I believe in persistence, confidence, a strong work ethic, building alliances, generosity towards strangers, and patience.

His advice for startups today: look at the big picture.

The $10 you spend to buy a domain name and the $5 a month you *might spend to host it could be the best investment you will ever make in your own future success: $70 a year could return control of your life to you. There is no better investment.*

Even if you are starting with someone else's affiliate program as your product, it is always better to direct your advertising to your own domain. Down the road, the affiliate program may be gone. The investment you make now can serve you well beyond whatever affiliate program you are promoting at the moment. Everyone has got to start somewhere, so promoting someone else's affiliate program may be a good start. But later on if you are keen to see what you are good at and what you enjoy doing, you may be able to develop your own programs, products, or services.

By promoting yourself from day one, through your own domain—even if it is only a storefront for an affiliate program—you will be laying the foundation that will help you today and tomorrow. When you promote yourself well on the Internet, chances are good that your promotional efforts are eternal. I still draw traffic and sales today from promotional materials I created for another program back in early 2000. The program is long gone, but my domain still pulls the traffic from that set of promotional materials and activities, and I am always able to convert some of that traffic into paying clients.

Jim Daniels

Jim Daniels began his online business with just $300, and six months later he quit his job to work on his online business full-time. His online income is now six figures a year. Jim's BusinessWeb2000, **www.businessWeb2000.com**, site shows others how to earn profits from the Web.

Jim's newest creation, **www.ezWebBusinessBuilder,** has been receiving great reviews from both newcomers to Internet marketing and Web marketing veterans. It is called the world's easiest solution for anyone interested in making their living online. Customers say there's really nothing else like it online. He has proven by his own example that fortunes are being made online, and everyday people can be part of it.

He wasn't always an expert Internet marketing consultant. He purchased his first computer in 1996 with a tax refund check. Then he spent his evenings searching for the best way to start an online business. "By the time I'd found my way around the Internet, I had 40 pages of great tips, a road map to starting a business online," he said.

Daniels's first publication, *Internet E-mail! Beyond the Basics*, now available online as an eBook, was based on 40 pages of tips to start an online business. Sales were so hot that he saw his career changing because he was making more from his Internet business than he was from his day job.

Words of advice: "Beware Overload."

The 'Net is a great place to learn about anything from aardvarks to zucchini. And while this information superhighway creates a great opportunity to discover new things, it comes as a bit of a double-edged sword. From day one it was inevitable that "information overload" would creep into the language, and it has. People are simply bombarded with information, and too much of a good thing can be bad. This trend will continue to grow, and if you're doing business on the Web, you need consider solutions not only for yourself but for your customers' peace of mind.

Here are some tips that will help you.

- *Make your information easy to locate on the Web and in your e-mail.*

- *Make your Web site a safe haven for frazzled Web surfers.*

- *Make sure your Ezine is one that gets read.*

Locating Key Information

When searching the Web, use effective search engines. For example, META engines search multiple search engines at once so you do not have to bounce from engine to engine. I use the multi-search engine Dogpile so much I posted a search tool, www.businessWeb2000.com/engines.htm at my site. It is ideal for finding things in a hurry.

Use your e-mail program as a powerful archive. This is as simple as saving every e-mail message you ever send. A program like Eudora is ideal for this. Simply create a mailbox called outgoing archive and rather than deleting old outgoing messages, transfer them all to this mailbox. People are amazed when you "recall" conversations you had with them years before. What you're really doing is using the powerful search tools that scans years of old messages in seconds. You can find conversations, old passwords, business deals, and any other detail in just seconds. Make your Web site a safe haven for visitors.

At your Web site tell your visitors why they should stay as soon as they arrive! Don't make your visitors guess what your site will do for them. Prominently display a reason for them to stick around. Most successful sites go as far as describing their site content right in their URL, so visitors know what to expect BEFORE they get to the site. If your URL doesn't do that, consider getting a few domains that do, then redirect them to your main site. Try my domain wizard www.businessWeb2000.com/wizard if you're looking for a great new domain name or two.

Once your visitor has arrived, direct them to the most popular areas of your site without delay. You have less than 20 seconds to make an impression. Most visitors will be gone if they have not found something of value within that time.

*Ask for a visitor's e-mail address as soon as they arrive. They'll love you for giving them a way to stay in touch, and your business will grow endlessly. Not asking right away was a mistake I was making for years. A recent adjustment at my home page, **www.businessWeb2000.com**, has doubled the number of subscribers to this newsletter each day. Consider this one-two punch of attention-grabbing and address-grabbing as critical to your long-term success.*

Be brief. Nearly everything you write at your site can be said with half the words. Remember, paragraphs that are longer than 60 words are too long, particularly on your main page. (This little paragraph is 60 words!) A wall of text scares Web surfers away. Stick to the point. Use bulleted lists if you can; they make for an easier read.

Make sure your Ezine is one that gets read. Describe each issue in the subject line. I learned this lesson personally. My own readership increased when I stopped naming each issue "BusinessWeb Gazette" and started telling my readers what each issue contained, right in the subject line. Don't wait to get your reader's attention. Grab it before they decide whether to open your message. Take a few minutes to name each issue with a subject that you yourself would be interested in. It should be intriguing and relevant to your subscribers.

Shorten your newsletter. I see more and more publishers streamlining their e-publications because of information overload. Even established Ezines like Chronicles are realizing that less is sometimes more. When subscribers have 100 messages waiting in their inbox, it is hard to set aside 15 minutes to read one newslet-

ter. Try to publish something that can be devoured in five minutes or less. A good rule of thumb is to keep it under 20k in size. Your readers will be more likely to read it from top to bottom and you'll earn a faithful following.

Jim's site has helped thousands of folks profit online. Visit **www.businessWeb2000.com** for FREE "how-to" cybermarketing assistance, software, manuals, and Web services. No time to visit the site? Subscribe to their free, weekly "BusinessWeb E-Gazette"; mail to www.freegazette@businessWeb2000.com.

Yanik Silver

Name: Yanik Silver

Web site: www.klausdahl.com/Yanik_Silver_Instant_Internet_Profits_review.htm

Yanik Silver is recognized as the leading expert in creating automatic, moneymaking Web sites, and he still doesn't know how to design a Web site. He is a direct response copywriter and marketing consultant who specializes in creating powerful tools and resources for entrepreneurs to enhance their businesses. He is the author, co-author, and/or creator of several best-selling online marketing books and tools including, *Instant Internet Profits, Surefire Sales Letter Secrets, The Ultimate Sales Letter Toolbox,* and *How to Cash in on More Cosmetic Patients.* His newest resource for making this year your best yet are at Sure Fire Marketing, **www.SureFireMarketing.com**.

He began his career selling medical equipment at 16 when he received his driver's license. A customer gave him his first taste of direct marketing and helped him discover what he wanted to do at a young age. Before he began his online business in 1998, Yanik had a successful copywriting and marketing business offline.

His most popular online work is *Instant Sales Letters*, which contains easy to use, fill-in-the-blank templates.

He wrote several marketing books including: *Surefire Sales Letter Secrets, The Ultimate Sales Letter Toolbox, 21 Mind Motivators: Psychological Tactics to Capture More Profits, Instant Sales Letters, Instant Internet Profits, 33 Days to Online Profits, 33 Days to Online Profits VIDEO Enhanced Tutorial eBook, Autoresponder Magic,* and *Million Dollar E-mails.*

What motivates this extremely successful businessman? The driving forces was his father. "My father has influenced my life the most. As a Russian immigrant, he came to this country with $356 in his pocket and within two years, he had started his own medical equipment sales and service business. Today it does $2.5 million annually. From him, I got the entrepreneurial spirit. In fact, one day, I'm going to write a book about the 'immigrant success secret' — why American born children are less likely to become millionaires than immigrants."

From his experience as a salesman he learned what elements made people buy — their "hot buttons" — then wrote about his findings to become the millionaire copywriter he is today.

His best advice can be found in an article he wrote and furnished for this interview:

How to Make This Year Your Best Year Ever©
By Yanik Silver

Every year I've been in business for myself online has been better than the year before. Recently, I decided to create an "Apprentice" program. (Yes, even before Trump.) I was extremely pleased that we had nearly 100 percent of my apprentices get an online venture up and running.

I've gone back and thought about their projects and how they developed, and I came to a striking conclusion that will be worth a lot of money to you this year if you heed it. There was one key aspect that got them off their butts and making money and it came down to one thing—a deadline!

As simple as that sounds, once a firm deadline was established, that's when the rubber met the road and all obstacles melted away like snow flakes in a frying pan. I'll give you a perfect example. For one apprentice we were going back and forth a bit tidying up the project and trying to get it out the door. Many times people can try to make everything too perfect, and it never gets out so we said we are launching this project at the LIVE Apprentice Summit. That was it, and that was final.

The date of the Summit was getting closer and closer and I could see this apprentice start to sweat a bit, but I made him make the commitment to this deadline publicly during our group call, and he couldn't back out now.

Fast forward to the day of his launch. He had multiple obstacles that would normally have put the project on hold but not now. With the firm deadline in place and the opportunity for him to be embarrassed, our fine apprentice finished his project. We hit the "send" button, and he made a tidy sum from a tiny list over the weekend. And this was just the start because his project has made well into the five figures already. Why did it get finished?

What's your deadline for your first project or your next project? Is it something that's in your head? Not a good idea. It's pretty easy to keep moving that forward or letting other things take precedence.

Who knows about your deadline, and who's going to hold you to it? In some cases it's not a good idea to share your deadline or goal with another person, especially if they're the negative energy vampire a lot of well-meaning friends and family turn out to be. But if you've got a group of colleagues all with the same thinking, use them. This works especially well if you don't want to look like an idiot in front of them and if they are people you really respect.

I'll tell you what works for me and maybe it'll work for you too. For me, I work best when I absolutely HAVE TO perform. For instance my first product on Internet marketing might never have been made (or at least it would have taken much longer) if I didn't sell it before it was done. When I first started marketing online in 2000, a lot of people wanted to know exactly what I did and how I started making money so fast.

I got my first opportunity to share my story in Atlanta at an Internet seminar. I was extremely nervous. My heart was beating out of my chest at the thought of talking in front of 100 strangers. I gave my presentation, and then I sold this product—yet to be created. I told people it would be delivered in a few weeks so they knew it was a prepublication offer. I walked away with 10 orders at $200 each. All well and good except I couldn't charge anyone until the manual was done. Even though it was only $2,000, minus what I had to pay the promoter.

I knew that at least people wanted this information and I could keep selling it once I finished it. I probably had a week or two of 3 a.m. work sessions, but I completed it and charged the cards. I was under pressure to get the manual done because these people paid me (though I didn't charge them) and I owed them the material. Since then I've updated my course material and it's been worth well into the six figures. It got done just because I had to do it.

How can you set something like this up for yourself? If you can stand the pressure, you can decide to put on a teleseminar. This is one of my favorite ways of creating product by a deadline. You can do either a one-time teleseminar or series of teleseminars, and you get paid to produce the product. How great is that? It doesn't matter if you have one person or 1000 people on the call because it forces you to create product and perform.

Once you've set your deadline for anything, you'll "magically" see certain resources fall into place. Trust me, it's a bit eerie but when it occurs every time you set a firm deadline, you know there's something to it. Just the act of making the decision sets these events into motion for you. It's also because what you focus on becomes your reality. Your perception has changed. Your internal "radar" is now attuned to resources and allies that can help you get your project completed.

Now I leave you with one more secret. Set "mini deadlines." When you're looking at the whole task of setting up an Internet business (or anything really) it's easy to get overwhelmed. But if you break everything up into small tasks with their own deadlines you'll be at your destination before you know it. I promise it'll work for you. In fact, that's one of the reasons I really like Franklin planner systems (now Franklin Covey). I've been using them since 1998, and that's when I first started making some significant changes in my life.

Actually the founder of Franklin, Mr. Hyrum Smith, has a great book called The 10 Essential Laws of Time and Life Management *which should be required reading for you! Even though I hate ad slogans because they don't work, this one should become your mantra for the year - "Just Do It." As cliché and overused as it is, that's all it comes down to—whether you're willing to roll the dice and put yourself out there a little. I promise whatever the worst case scenario you're thinking, it is far from the reality.*

If you need someone to send your deadline list to, go ahead and e-mail it to me. I'll keep it confidential, and we'll celebrate together when you reach your destination.

Chad Tackett

Chad Tackett, creator/president of Global Health Fitness, is an innovator in the integrated, non-diet approach to health and fitness. He is the author of all five "Global Health & Fitness" components (online books) and designed all of the customized strength training, flexibility training, and cardiovascular exercise programs. He has trained and educated people in exercise and nutrition for more than eight years.

Chad has a Bachelor of Science degree in Exercise and Sport Science from Oregon State University and is certified as a professional personal trainer and weight management specialist. Additional professional education includes several dozen personal trainer/health-and-fitness seminars taught by professionals from around the world, including "Heart Zone Training" from Sally Edwards and "Shaping the Future of Exercise" with Dr. James Peterson and Dr. Cedric Bryant.

You'll find more about him at your online guide to healthy living and optimal fitness, **www.global-fitness.com/fitnessconsultants/tackett.php,** and more about his programs at **www.global-fitness.com/membership.html**.

My background is fitness, and I owned a health club at the time I began to understand the power and potential of the Internet in 1996. I sold my club and spent a year developing the content for my online fitness program. In April 1997, I went online and began making a profit two months later. It's snowballed from there.

Our only product was the "GHF Online Fitness Program." Take

*our brief video Web site tour at www.global-fitness.com/
sitetour.php to learn more.*

Once again, key characteristics Chad believes were most beneficial
are a strong belief in yourself and the willingness to work hard
consistently.

His advice for startups today:

> *After you get your site up, you need to get qualified buyers to it.
> As far as marketing, there are three main ways we get people to
> our site:*

> - *Search Engine Optimization. Let me know if you'd like
>   my SEO specialists' contact information. I recommend
>   an effective, excellent affiliate program such as Isocracy.*
>
> - *Partnerships with similar sites where we offer their site
>   free but require a credit line with our link.*
>
> - *I never had to spend a cent on advertising because of the
>   strategies implemented.*

Denise Hall

Denise Hall is the owner of Home Business on a Budget, **www.
home-business-on-a-budget.com,** and several other Web sites.
Her goal is to help new and intermediate marketers find the tools
and resources they need for their business without spending an
arm and a leg.

> *I started online in the fall of 2002. For the first few months I just
> read anything and everything I could get my hands on to try to
> learn how to market online. In January 2003 I started writing
> articles and submitting them to Ezines to brand my name. I also*

started publishing my own Ezine, Home Business on a Budget Newsletter, *at about that time.*

The first, and so far the only, paid product I've created was an eBook called Get Inside the Minds of Scam Artists! Discover the Tricks of Their Trade!

Two of my online friends both lost money when customers ripped them off. The customers made the purchase through PayPal and ClickBank but then reported to those companies that they'd never purchased from my friends. I hate seeing people get scammed so I wrote the eBook.

It made me realize how easy it is for people to request refunds online fraudulently, so I decided I had to let business owners know how to fight back if it ever happens to them.

What has made her successful?

I think there are several elements. First, my personality—I'm not a quitter, so I just kept plugging away at it. I was determined to succeed and get out of my stressful day job. Second, I met a lot of good people online who were very helpful in answering questions and offering help. Third, I started paying more attention to those who were already successful. I've tried to learn from them by visiting their Web sites and reading their e-mails and their opt-in lists. And last, I took action on what I learned. I think that's the most important part. Learning what to do isn't the same as actually doing it.

What advice does she have for new or would-be 'netrepreneurs?

I'd tell people to learn as much as possible and practice what you learn as soon as you learn it. Don't worry that something won't work for you. Try it and see. Just take action or you will never get anywhere. Don't ever think you can't do something. If you need help, ask a friend. There are plenty of people online who are willing to answer questions and teach you how to do things.

Never give up on your dreams of becoming successful. The only thing holding you back is you.

Donesia Muhammad

Donesia Muhammad is the co-owner of KDM Publishing, which specializes in e-mail marketing, article marketing, promotion, Web design, and development. They started with one site and have expanded into several Web sites. You can find them at **www.DonesiaMuhammad.com**, **www.EzineAdHelper.com**, and **www.ReprintedArticles.com**.

Donesia's story:

I think I was meant to be a business owner. I have always had the entrepreneurial spirit in me but when I researched the start-up costs, that put the brakes on starting a business. Then I realized how much cheaper it was to open a business online. I started to get interested in the 'Net in 2000, realizing that as a stay-at-home Mom of three children, I wanted to keep myself occupied and make an extra income. I had a computer that a relative gave me, and it was a challenge since I had never been online before. I am old school when it came to computer technology. My heyday was when Basic was the programming language and my big old computer was an Atari, Commodore 64 or Radio Shack TRS-80. Needless to say, I had a long way to go as I taught myself. Crash your computer a few times and see how much you can learn! After reading several books from the library and surfing through the Internet, I knew I was ready to start a business.

I began an e-mail newsletter in November 2001 called My iBusiness Weekly, *www.myibusinessweekly.com, which is* *still going strong today. My first official site was Ezine Ad Helper, **www.Ezineadhelper.com**, which is a newsletter co-op advertising site. At that point, I was hooked. In February 2002 I purchased my business license and launched Ezine Ad Helper, and I haven't looked back. At first, my family thought I was going crazy with the computer. My husband thought maybe this was a fad and I would get bored with it. Now he is hooked too. He saw what I can accomplish online from home and knew our future was to own an online business. I have since expanded with these sites: **www. KDMPublishing.com**, **www.ReprintedArticles.com**, and **www.DonesiaMuhammad.com**. I have more coming next year.*

My main focus has always been advertising. I have loved advertising since I was a child. I'm fascinated by it. Once I knew that I was a good salesperson, I wanted advertising to be my main focus. My first love has always been writing, and I know how to use words to my advantage. Article marketing is big business these days. Over the past few years I have seen it grow tremendously online. I knew it was the perfect time to fine-tune my writing skills and make it work for me. That included sales copy, eBook writing, and article distribution—the works. Soon people realized that content is king, that the search engines love to see content not just junk on Web sites. Article writing increased. I used that knowledge along with my advertising expertise to make it work for my clients and me.

I went through a long period of trying to find my niche. I had expertise in a lot of different fields, but they weren't bringing in sales or creating a good business reputation. Although I now realize that advertising and promotion are my niche, there are so many aspects that comprise that field. There are many things that I am learning, such as software development to enhance and strengthen my abilities further.

What does she attribute her success to today?

Learning how to balance it all. I didn't think I could do this at first, having two children and a house and a business. I put off school and everything else because I thought it was all too much. It was time to make a list of priorities and realize that if I didn't start this business now, it would never happen. I kept my family intact by balancing my daily duties and sticking to a schedule that works for me.

Now that I have my business, I am back in school online (I'll graduate in a few months), and I just had my third child this year. My husband comes up with business strategies, and we are a winning team. Now my daughters want to start their own Internet business, following in Mom's footsteps. So it is the support of my family that has helped make our online business a success.

The best advice I can give someone is to make your business work for you. Don't assume you can be like everyone else. What works for them may not work for you. People will tell you that it was super easy to start their business. Most of the time, these people are the ones trying to sell you something. They tell you how they made millions in months. They don't tell you how much invest-ment money they started with or how many people helped them out in the beginning. If you have young children, family and/or job obligations, understand that it will take time. Don't try to be super human or before you realize it, you'll have lost the job that was paying your bills, your children don't mind you because you've neglected them, and your spouse has left.

I knew when it was time to take a break. When I had my third child this year, I wondered how I was going to run my business and take care of a newborn. So I scaled back the company, automated most of my tasks, and I stopped publishing my newsletter until the baby was six weeks old. I took it easy. I knew what my priorities were because you don't get those early months back with a child.

Running a business is a wonderful goal, but you don't have to be the next Bill Gates or Google within thirty days to be successful. Success isn't always measured by your bank account. So wake up and smell the roses instead of smelling that old coffee sitting by your computer.

Theresa Cahill

Theresa Cahill has more than 20 years' experience in marketing and is the owner of "My Wizard Ads," **www.mywizardads.com**, an online advertising co-op specializing in Ezine advertising, solo ads, and targeted traffic, all at prices almost anyone can afford.

In 1990 after almost a year online playing games and doing ridiculous things like clicking little downloaded programs for pennies, in disgust, I created a Web site strictly for my own amusement. It was the former The Wizard's World of Strange and Unusual Choices. *To tell others about it and not having a clue how to "advertise," I wrote to the 13 people in my address book and asked them to go take a look. In that same e-mail, I threw in a few "strange and unusual" items. They came, they looked, and they didn't refuse to receive my brand new "newsletter." A Web site and Ezine was born.*

One of the greatest ways to grow the circulation for your newsletter is to trade Ezine ads with other publishers. By September 1991, I was trading ads with approximately 150 publishers. It was its own edition! I then had the thought that at least some of those publishers might like to work with me in a cooperative fashion so I created the Web site, "My Wizard Ads." Working together with publishers around the world to provide great resources for marketers and advertisers is a mutual arrangement that really works.

Now keeping in mind that successful is a relative word, I think what brings people back to "My Wizard Ads" is the fact that I am

*ponding to e-mails or taking the time to call an adver-
/ possible, when there is a question. This customer service
ramount to surviving online. Nothing is worse than ordering
so.nething and having no one acknowledge that you did. Being
available and being helpful are critical to online success.*

What advice does she have for startups?

*Don't join anything and don't spend money anywhere until you
absolutely feel certain you understand what you're getting into.
You need to know for sure whether you're 100 percent positive you
will give it your all. Do not believe you can make something from
nothing. It doesn't work in the real world, and it most certainly will
not work online. Don't be a sucker. I've spoken with too many individuals who have thrown money away without once understanding what was involved. This adage is true: If it sounds too good to
be true, it probably is. Be smart. Research. Read. Ask questions!*

Doug Williams

Name: Doug Williams
Web site: www.viralhost.com/cgi-bin/refer.cg

*I started my online experience on April 1, 1997. I'd heard that people
could make money on the 'Net, and since I have four children and
was too ill to leave the house to work, I had no options.*

*I soon found out that 99.9 percent of the people offering to "show
me how" were only proficient in showing me how they would
relieve me of my money. I spent a full year, 12 to 15 hours a day,
and a lot of money I couldn't afford to discover this harsh reality.*

*Make no mistake, success online is tough for the little guy. Most
sites on the 'Net are backed by big business, and their first and
last consideration is the bottom line, the profit margin. I've seen a*

number of small operators with good ideas get impatient for their success to happen and bring in outside investors. Big mistake. They lost control of their dream and never reached success. It took me seven years to get where I am today, a mid-range six-figure income, a successful registered company with several employees and thousands of the finest people on the planet as members of our programs.

The benefit to you covers many levels. The key, the anchor to online success, the only commodity that makes or breaks any online success, is people. You can have the best idea, the greatest deal, or finest product in the world, but without people you have nothing.

Since the first day I logged onto the 'Net, I made myself a personal commitment to keep my business honest at any cost. That caused some turmoil in my life in the form of threats, attempted lawsuits, and slander. Still, I have not swayed from my course. I have been instrumental in bringing down a number of bogus or scam programs, not by lying, but just by identifying and exposing wrongs most people already knew about and tried to ignore. People left our programs, but the honest, quality people stayed and flourished.

Keep your focus. If you haven't been online before, you need to look at your plans, anchor yourself with perseverance, focus, and persistence. Otherwise, you will fail. No, I'm not talking negatively, but realistically. If you follow our program training, you will start to enjoy a growing level of success.

Once you start becoming recognized for your success, lazy folk pour out of every crack on the planet. There are literally millions who want to make it to the "big time" without actually working for it. Once you establish that you are a team builder and a seasoned online marketer, they want you because you just might make them rich overnight.

So the offers start pouring in: SPAM, phone calls, faxes, snail mail. Some people may actually knock on your door. Heck, some might even be long lost friends. Over the years I've seen some good folk leave our programs and go for that brass ring only to land on their heads. The smart ones don't quit; they just come back to us with more determination than ever. Sadly, many just get offline altogether and often with strained finances. Remember this thought: If it's not as good a deal next week as it supposedly is today, there is no deal.

Doug Williams started with a network marketing opportunity at **www.3step.com/cgi-bin/refer.cgi** in 1998. Late in 2001 he started "Viral Visitors," a traffic program, at a time when many people used traffic programs, and then he added three more. He now has several network marketing opportunities that emphasize making money by being a team player. His main business is a hosting company called ViralHOST.com, **www.viralhost.com/cgi-bin/refer.cgi**. Doug is all about honesty, perseverance, and working together.

Dave MacGregor

Name: Dave MacGregor
E-mail: davem@easyebookcreator.com
Phone: 206-337-1782

Dave MacGregor started his Internet career in 2002 when the software house he was working for unexpectedly closed. Having worked in both programming and sales for the American computer giant, NCR, he was ideally suited to business online.

Understanding that the Internet is all about information, he concentrated his efforts on publishing products and software. His first success was the eBook compiler, "Easy Ebook Creator" and then the newsletter/Ezine creator 123Ezine.

Today, many products later, Dave realizes the difficulty faced by Internet beginners and is releasing a raft of new products to demystify the intricacies of doing business online to sell that first eBook.

Here are Dave's candid words on his success and some tips to help others to succeed.

How did he begin his online business?

I was really forced into starting an online business in April 2002 when the company I was working for closed. It was a software house that developed solutions for local governments but found they were not big enough to keep up with the changes in both technology and political requirements—a common fate of online businesses.

I started off with a product named "Instant Web Sites" which I had branded for me; that is, I had it renamed "Easy Mini Sites." It creates your mini Web site, a sales and "thank you" page and links it into the payment processor, Clickbank. It was an easy way to use a software product that anyone wanting to sell online would need. However, not knowing anything at that time about generating traffic, I pulled it because it only sold a few copies.

I also felt that branding other peoples products was not the way to go because it did not allow me to satisfy my customers' demands for more product features. I had no means to change or enhance the product, leaving me high and dry—not a recipe for a successful future.

Armed with those thoughts, I had come across a number of software products that did a good job but looked a little untidy and needed a face lift. One was an eBook compiler and the other a text Ezine creator—you've guessed it—"EasyEbookCreator" and the original "123Ezine." I hunted down and negotiated with both authors and bought the complete rights including source code to the software. "EasyEbookCreator" was born and today I have more than 10,000 users mostly sold through affiliates/resellers.

What key personal elements aided in his success?

I am not the sharpest tack in the box, but I make up for it in other ways—tenacity, for one. I go at things doggedly and rarely do I give up. Now this approach has its drawbacks not the least being that you can have your head so far up your proverbial that you can't see where you're going, so I try to have someone to bounce my ideas around with or to talk to when I get bogged down.

I also take action in that I do not just talk a good game like so many people do. That said, I have bought loads of products and done absolutely nothing with them. However, if I felt they had merit and were appropriate and complementary to what I was trying to do, I would use them. The biggest problem I find about taking action is that I can end up doing too many things at the one time. I am a sucker for getting side-tracked, another reason to have a buddy to help me stay focused.

Finally, I don't get embarrassed. Maybe I am just thick-skinned or some would say "thick." What I mean is that I know I have to learn constantly and I am not afraid to ask. It's the only way to be when you're a one-man business.

What is his key advice for newcomers?

If I were to start over again, I would not get involved in writing software as I did (my background was in software). Yes, what I am saying is that I would not do what I am currently doing and what has made me successful! Why? Because software has to be supported, and to provide quality support takes a lot of time and effort, and that's what I spend a lot of my time on. However, if I wrote and sold e-books, I would be providing little support and handling few if any technical issues, and that would provide me with either a heck of a lot more leisure time or income depending how I played it. I'm still learning, obviously.

Trademark Productions, Inc.

Name: Trademark Publications
Web site: www.tmprod.com
E-mail: sales@tmprod.com

The idea for Trademark Productions, Inc., was born more than 14 years ago as a simple side-business aimed at serving the music and graphic art industries. Dwight Zahringer, Trademark's founder and president, was studying graphic and commercial art along with desktop publishing when the opportunity to expand into music and entertainment marketing presented itself.

Trademark spent the next few years promoting major music acts such as Moby, Britney Spears, and Creed, as well as artists from labels such as Warner Brothers, Universal, Hollywood, Sony, Mercury, and TVT Records. Trademark worked with numerous recording companies to promote their artists across the United States.

This promotion expanded into retail environments aimed at direct markets and expanded beyond music to include print magazines such as *URB*, shoe companies like Pony Shoes, and consumer brands like Purina Beneful and Coca-Cola.

The focus of Trademark soon shifted, though, when the Internet revolution began taking hold in the mid-1990s. The worlds of entertainment marketing, Web site design, and graphic design were changing rapidly, and it became obvious that Trademark was going to have to keep up with the new developments to thrive. Since that time, Trademark Productions has expanded their services to include a Web site development company that specializes in search engine ranking to help your Web site be placed under the right keywords on search engines. TM can help bring qualified traffic to your Web site.

Because TM was involved in the Internet game from such an early stage, the company has had the privilege of watching it develop. That background and experience allows TM to offer customers the very best in online business consulting, search engine placement (SEO), ranking, and Web site development. TM knows what works on the Web and what doesn't. TM is constantly learning about new technologies and is dedicated to using that knowledge to assist clients. Today, Trademark offers Web site development, SEO optimization, online business consulting, and online marketing services.

The growth and development of Trademark Productions has been quite extensive since a small, one-man operation was launched in 1991. Trademark is now a flourishing team of professional Web site developers, SEO copywriters, and online marketing specialists.

During the interview with one of Trademark's founding members, Pete Garbowski, we asked about the biggest obstacle encountered in the effort to launch their online venture. He said that it was establishing an appealing price while building a reputation on value and customer service.

What are the key personal elements he felt were most important in the success of Trademark Publications?

Personal attention to customer service, customer satisfaction, and customer loyalty have built Trademark's business to the level of success it enjoys, and none of that would have been possible without careful attention and perseverance in creating a product that satisfied the customers.

What advice does he have for startup entrepreneurs?

Plan, persevere, give your customers what they want, and don't try to diversify and grow too quickly.

Web Advantage, Inc.

Name: Web Advantage, Inc.
Web site: www.Webadvantage.net
E-mail: bonniejones@gmail.com

Ms. Hollis Thomases, president and founder of WebAdvantage. net has an extensive 19-year background in sales and marketing. WebAdvantage.net is an interactive marketing, promotions, and advertising agency specializing in building and implementing Internet strategies to acquire and retain qualified Web site visitors.

Its core competencies include search engine optimization, producing online advertising campaigns, and managing opt-in e-mail marketing campaigns. *Forbes* magazine recognized the company Web site, **www.Webadvantage.net**, as one of its "Best of B2B Sites" for media and advertising. An award-winning entrepreneur and graduate of Cornell University, Ms. Thomases has been named to Baltimore's "40 Under 40" in 2003 and was the sole recipient of the 2002 Bush Declaration Award for Entrepreneurial Spirit.

Hollis currently writes a bi-weekly column, "Online Media Buying Agency Strategies," as contributing columnist for ClickZ and a quarterly column for National Hotel Executive. She has also been recognized on CNNfn.com, has appeared on TechTV's "Working the Web," and in *The Baltimore Sun, Success Magazine, Catalog Age,* and *iMarketing News*. She has also made presentations at conferences for such organizations as Incisive Media (search engine strategies), the Kelsey Group, the American Marketing Association, ClickZ, the Newsletter and Electronic Publishers Association, the Dingman Center for Entrepreneurship, and the Direct Marketing Association of Washington, DC.

She has served on several advisory boards: Association for Interactive Marketing's Online Promotions Council; Maryland Business Roundtable for Education's Teen Web Project; Harford County Economic Development Advisory Board, and Harford County's Small Business Development Center. She co-founded the Digital Bridge Initiative, a philanthropic outreach venture between the Greater Baltimore Technology Council (GBTC), of which she is an active participant, and the non-profit community. She is also a member of the philanthropic giving circle, the B'More Fund. She lives in Delaware with her husband and enjoys the company of friends, fitness, dance, dining of any kind, and reading.

This is Ms. Thomases' story:

> *In 1998, I realized that Web entities were going to need the same marketing as their earthly counterparts and felt I could help fill the void. My original concept was to promote Web businesses through shared cost-print advertising (co-op ads). Though my idea was met with interest, my prospects seemed even more interested in marketing their Web sites directly online. Though I knew nothing of how to execute this marketing at the time, I recognized a good*

opportunity when I saw one and quickly went to work learning how to do online marketing while I took a hiatus from selling my co-op print advertising concept.

Back then, there was very little means to learn online marketing other than to roll up your sleeves and do it. There were a few printed books, no university courses—mostly you just searched online, subscribed to a lot of newsletters and e-mail lists, asked a lot of questions, and practiced what you absorbed. Using my own Web site as a guinea pig, I tested the theories and tactics I was learning, and by the time someone contacted me to do for them what I was doing for my own site, I felt I was ready to relaunch WebAdvantage.net as the business it is today. That whole process took about four months.

Why did she start her own business?

My entrepreneurial drive and spirit needed an outlet. I come from an entrepreneurial family, and it was a life-long aspiration of mine to own my own business. I'm the person who has an idea a day, and I had a huge file of business ideas that I had killed for one reason or another.

Before starting WebAdvantage, I was working in the traditional marketing world. When the Internet came along, I felt it was going to be big, but I didn't know how I could tap into it if I wasn't a computer programmer or graphic designer. It wasn't until my epiphany about the marketing of Web sites hit me that I realized how I could apply my sales and marketing skills to the Internet world. My idea was so good, I thought, and my belief in the Internet so strong that I literally had a crossing-the-chasm moment and knew I could quit my job and succeed against all odds.

Interestingly, the first successes I had were with online public relations. I understood how to use e-mail lists, message boards, and forums (predecessors to today's online social communities like MySpace) to get attention and build awareness.

But our real sweet spot was realized with search engine optimization (SEO). We were doing SEO even before Google existed! Though in those early days I could not so easily substantiate the impact top search engine rankings had on a client in terms of increases in site traffic or online sales. We knew that both were positively affected and so did our clients. SEO was also relatively easier to explain and sell—most people at least knew what a search engine was—than services like online PR, e-mail marketing, or site linking.

My biggest obstacle was that very few people could wrap their heads around the notion of online marketing. Everyone was too busy talking about building Web sites; very few people understood that the old adage, "Build it and they will come" does not apply on the Web. I was constantly having to explain that, "No, my company does not build Web sites," and after that, I would have to educate them as to what exactly Web marketing was and what it could do. It was a constant uphill battle to just break through to a level that people could comprehend. It's better today, but there are still a good many people who don't understand Web marketing.

I credit my success to a few factors:

- *I got in at the right time. The need for skilled Internet marketing was just being realized by corporate marketing professionals.*

- *I did a good job at positioning myself as an expert. I did a lot of writing, public speaking, and my own public relations.*

- *I sought help from those with skill sets better than my*

own. Why waste my time and energy on accounting, contract negotiations, and bookkeeping when they don't contribute to my company's growth if I feel obliged to do them myself?

- *I was able to surround myself with a team whom I trusted to help make the business grow.*

- *I worked really hard.*

- *I got lucky.*

- *I thanked everyone who helped me, even in the tiniest way. A little thank you goes a long way!*

What is her advice to newcomers?

The online world is a far more populous, complex place than it used to be, but I would say that building a solid team of advisors, professional service providers, and staff is critical to your success. Be prepared to work really hard and don't expect it to come easy. Also, if you're in it for the long haul, plan for a rainy day. (Think Dot-Com Bust).

Services

SUCCESS STORIES

In this section we feature successful businesses that provide all sorts of services to consumers every day. In the Success Stories, we've included examples of businesses running dual operations: retail and online. These business people have discovered what you may one day understand: a dual operation can increase sales in both areas!

Barbara Jennings

*I'm the CEO of **decorate-redecorate.com**, an online training site for anyone wishing to learn how to arrange furniture professionally, become an interior redesigner or home staging professional, or learn how to become a corporate art consultant. We are the world's largest, most trusted redesign training center. You can tailor our training courses to fit your needs, and we provide on-going support and guidance. I've personally owned my own businesses since 1972 and am a firm believer in the entrepreneurial spirit.*

Her first online business was started in October 2002 with the two products, "Decor Secrets Revealed" and "Where There's a Wall—There's a Way."

What does she feel are the personal characteristics for success?

First, it's nice if you have background and experience in some aspect of life that you enjoy and that you feel other people can use for their benefit.

You have to publicize and market products and services that other people want or need, or no one will know about them. Then you have to create a product or service that has high value, quality, and benefits and back it with a great guarantee and customer service.

You have to be tenacious, believe in yourself, and never give up.

You need to be trained in the concepts of Internet marketing, which are different from offline marketing. It helps greatly to have the right training and the right software to manage your business. Not all trainers are good so you have to separate the good from the bad. But most of all, you have to study and apply what you learn. So many people buy training and never do anything with it and then wonder why they fail.

While the Internet business is, in my opinion, the greatest business anyone can get into, it does take hard work and perseverance—something many, many people are unwilling to do. There is a huge learning curve to overcome, usually, and if people can't get past their fear of learning something new and different, and if they don't have the work ethic to apply what they learn, they will fail. Nothing great happens overnight, and most people have unrealistic dreams and are unwilling to back them up with good, old-fashioned hard work.

What is her advice for beginners?

I would go to the link below for my training. I would buy the "Insider Secrets Marketing Course" to teach you all about Internet marketing concepts no matter why type of business you want to start. It's where I got my training and most of my software to manage my business. They have great support staff and are wonderful people. They were instrumental in helping me achieve my comfortable six-figure income.

Portraits in Determination

Name of company: Portraits in Determination

Date started: March 1999

Web site: www.portraitsindetermination.com

Associate companies: www.indaFuriate.com, Linda Furiate Company

E-mail: LMFuriate@comcast.net

Ms. Linda Furiate was born in Frankfurt, Germany, daughter of a retired U.S. Army sergeant. Following in her father's footsteps she joined the U. S. Air Force after graduating from high school. She soon found herself stationed in Misawa, Japan, working with sensitive crypto logic intelligence and attending the University of Maryland. Upon completion of her tour of duty in Japan, Linda was stationed at Ft. Meade, Maryland, headquarters for an intelligence command located midway between Baltimore, Maryland, and Washington, D.C. After completing a six-year tour of duty, she left the Air Force and began a career in sales and marketing. In 1995, her career was abruptly halted when she was involved in a car accident. Shortly thereafter, she was diagnosed with a rare, incurable, neurological movement disorder called cervical dystonia. Earlier that year she had begun to be interested in Astrology and now works full-time as an astrological coach.

Linda is a noted teacher, astrologer, philosopher, author, coach, mentor, and talk show host inspiring others to conquer their own adversity and discover their true self. She has studied the works of many well known astrologers: Noel Tyl, Marion March, Joan McEvers, Maritha Pottenger, and she has trained under Louise Hay to become a prosperity workshop facilitator. Linda offers astrological coaching services to people who have suffered adversity and wish to overcome this portion of their journey to find real happiness and prosperity. She is also highly creative with an intense need to be a leader and to be independent in following a path to facilitate positive outcomes.

She created *Portraits in Determination* to use as a platform to help others, and that is how her online business began.

> *Initially the concept of* Portraits in Determination *started out as a cable access television show. My goal with the show was to talk to people who had experienced some adversity and setback and discuss how they were able to get through that period in their lives spiritually and emotionally. When I wasn't able to market the TV show as I had wanted but still had a great desire to help people, I decided to begin coaching people through their rough times and using astrology as a guide into their soul. I felt putting together a Web site to market my services was essential plus I knew it would open up a national market.*

> *I still produce and host the TV show that is mainly shown on my local cable access channel. However, episodes can be viewed on my Web site at* **www.portraitsindetermination.com.**

> *I was motivated to develop* Portraits in Determination, *the television show and astrological coaching after experiencing a disabling condition, cervical dystonia, which left me almost bedridden and housebound for more than two years. During that time I wasn't able to work outside my home but knew I still needed to*

*generate income to survive and support myself and my son. I felt
very fortunate because the whole time I was experiencing these
major setbacks both physically and financially I decided I would
look at each step of my journey and decide what I wanted to learn
and how I wanted to grow from my experiences. I felt in the back
of my mind that one day I would be called to share my experiences
and help others who were suffering.*

*My new ambition started off very slowly, so to pay the bills
I also began offering business services to include writing client
testimonials and Web content for small business owners plus
some other administrative tasks that I no longer do. The business
services took off quite well and have provided me with revenue
to fund additional marketing opportunities for the astrological
coaching aspect of my businesses. I still write the client testimonials and Web content. I have also had success marketing my book,*
101 Simple Suggestions and Quotations to Express Compas-
sion and Empathy.

Linda's physical limitation was not her biggest obstacle in establishing
her business. Her greatest need was funding.

*Of course I struggled with this, but it wasn't for a lack of moti-
vation or desire. My struggles when I first started my company
were mainly on a physical level. Because I was still healing my
body from severe symptoms, which include muscle spasms and
twisting of my upper torso I couldn't sit up in a chair or even hold
up my head to sit at my computer or talk on the phone. I had to
plan each and every moment of my day around my health. Some
days I could work for hours while others I may get two or three
minutes of comfort to perform the tasks necessary to do my job.
Over the years my symptoms have come and gone, so I just take
one moment at a time doing the things necessary to create the
success I desire. As of this writing I am doing extremely well and
working full-time.*

Her personal characteristics and key elements that have contributed to her success: discipline and intuition. After high school graduation I spent six years in the US Air Force. While there I developed a very structured and disciplined approach to life which now allows me to work well independently. I also have the ability to understand and feel a person's emotions and break them down so that the person can really understand and learn who they are. I am intuitive and am an effective communicator with a diplomatic nature and personality that hopefully keeps me from offending anyone.

> *I continue to study astrology each and every day reading as many books and Web sites that I can get my hands on. There is an infinite amount of information available, and I never know what I am going to need to know when working with a client. I want to know how and where to resource the necessary information to give a more accurate and in-depth reading.*

Her advice to beginners?

> *If you can tolerate working for someone else with a steady income, do it. Life provides much more stability when you don't find your self waking up every morning unemployed until you can make your own money for the day. If you are 100 percent self motivated and have the discipline to do what is necessary generate the income you desire by offering a product or service you love, then I would suggest starting off small when considering an online business. Do it in your spare time while still maintaining a steady income. When the online business is able to support you financially on its own then the time may be right to leave your day job and focus solely on a business that you love. If you don't love what you are doing you won't have the motivation and discipline to get out of bed each morning to conquer the world one sale at a time.*

Business Design Studio

Name of company: Business Design Studio

Date started: 1995

Web site: www.businessdesignstudio.com

Associate companies: www.digitalphotocollages.com
www.homebusinesswear.com

E-mail: info@businessdesignstudio.com

Eileen Parzek is an award-winning designer and writer providing graphic design and Web design services. Her company, Business Design Studio, **www.businessdesignstudio.com**, helps small businesses make a big impression, increase their reach, and grow. Located in Albany, New York, she has worked virtually and from home for companies around the world since 1995.

Eileen can always be found at the intersection of creativity, information, and technology. She has applied her talents to supporting the success of hundreds of small businesses and organizations around the world. She enjoys writing about computers from the human perspective and teaching people how to harness today's technology in their business and personal life.

She writes frequently for online publications and publishes a monthly newsletter entitled *Increase Your Reach: Infuse Your Marketing with Technology*. She has been featured in Albany City business journals, *Entrepreneur* magazine, and the National Federation of Independent Businesses publication, the American Express Platinum publication, *Home Business Magazine*, and *The Tech Valley Times*. She has also been interviewed for radio programs.

Here is her story:

In the early 90s, I was a dreadfully underpaid government worker, extremely unhappy in my job because I was doing things that civil service didn't recognize as a job. I had taught myself an assortment of computer and graphic design skills, like desktop publishing, how to code hypertext documents, how to design multimedia presentations with audio and animation, and how to create computer graphics. In 1995, a sympathetic co-worker called me to his cube to "see something amazing" and he showed me the World Wide Web, as it was back then. I was blown away by the potential when I saw how information, interconnected with hypertext, was being displayed in this networked format.

I literally ran home and started teaching myself how to create my own Web site. Back then most Web sites were gray with text, and the ability to put a graphic on a Web site was brand new. Since I was an artist with computer graphics skills, the little site I made was pretty high end for it's time! I began communicating with other people who were doing Web design and they were really awestruck by my work. Almost everyone online at the time—and there weren't very many—had a programming background so my design skills stood out, and people started asking me to jazz up their Web sites. Before long I had more to do than I could accomplish by staying up all night, and it started to affect my day job. Since I hated my job, it wasn't long before the boss confronted me and I resigned.

From there, I just flew by the seat of my pants. I had absolutely no business background, and everything I did I learned by doing. I changed my business model in 2003 to include print graphic design as well, so that I could help my clients more in their marketing design needs.

Her motivation came from her love of the work.

It really was that I had an assortment of skills that made absolutely no sense to anyone—and the day I saw the Web, I realized what I was supposed to be doing. I never intended or wanted to own a business. I literally was just doing what I loved, following the intuitive direction of my natural abilities, and I woke up one day and said, "Whoops! I haven't been to work in ages." Of course, 11 years later, I can hardly imagine any other way of working.

Her first success?

My Web site design was first, but that is really a service. I've enhanced my Web site with information products for "do it your-selfers" without any design background. I've written e-books for them, so that they don't make any huge mistakes in their journey. This was a smart move, because it meant that I had something to offer the people who came to my site just looking for free or cheap advice, not to hire me as a designer.

The most successful online venture, in terms of reach and popularity, has been **HomeBusinessWear.com**, *a Web site I created to celebrate the work-at-home lifestyle. It features t-shirts, hats, bags, and other merchandise with fun sayings and cartoon artwork. Since 54 percent of the small business population in the United States is home-based, I've done well with that Web site. It has also received publicity in terms of radio and magazine exposure.*

Her biggest obstacle was her lack of business background.

Yes, the biggest obstacle was usually ME! Since I didn't have a clue about business ownership and no training or education, I had to learn ALL my lessons the hard way. Her personal contributions to success?

Extreme creativity certainly had a big hand in my success. It allows me to cook up new schemes and brainstorms for self-promotion to attract new customers. I am very independent and self motivated.

I don't like having restrictions and limitations placed on what I can do so self-employment suits me just fine.

Discipline is important, especially when you work from a home studio as I do.

I'm also very resilient—I always bounce back. A good sense of humor keeps me amused by the whole experience, and a strong stomach allows me to survive the perilous financial rollercoaster.

And her advice to you?

Oh! Plan, plan, plan. I didn't, and it led to a lot of insanity. Know who your customers are, what your products and services are, and how you will stay afloat financially until you are making money. You'll be so much more successful (and sane) if you don't fly by the seat of your pants the way I did.

Don't fall for every product and service that promises a quick path to success online. Odds are they are just skilled copy writers who have learned how to "hook" you and separate you from your money. There are NO fast, easy, quick, or fool-proof plans–it takes persever-ance, hard work, planning, and strategy. Read lots of reviews and ask questions of others who have come before you before sending anyone $197 for the solution to all of your products.

Have money in the bank. The best way to start an online business is while you're already working somewhere else. Ramp up and when you're established and successful, you can leave your other job. Whatever you think you need to survive on, and however long you expect it will take to be a success, multiply it by two, or better yet, three times.

The Home Business People, Inc.

Name: Jenn Bonoff

Location: Middletown, RI

Web site: www.ZeroToSixFigures.com

E-mail: grouper@bonoff.com

Phone: 401-849-2639

Type of business: Author, Home-Business Consultant, Web Site Designer & Internet Marketer

I began my first Internet business in August 2000, and now I have multiple online businesses that I own and operate. I am the author of a 224-page, soft-covered book titled, Zero to Six Figures. *My book tells the story of how I started my own Internet-based business from home at the age of 24 with virtually no experience or capital to invest. It details my rise to success and guides readers through the process of successfully starting and operating home-based businesses of their own. I also have a Web site design business that provides affordable Web sites to both traditional and home-based businesses.*

*Last, I operate **SportsToSchool.com** which helps high school athletes promote themselves to college coaches.*

As far back as I can remember, I had a drive to choose a different path. I didn't want my life to be ordinary but exhilarating and fresh. I am an entrepreneur, and I always wanted a business of my own. I had no idea what my future would hold after graduating from Yale. I didn't send out my resume and go to interviews as my classmates were doing. My family thought I was crazy for not even looking for a job. I didn't put together a resume or write a cover letter. Imagine the shock—over $130,000 for an ivy-league education, and I certainly didn't appear to be headed down the "right" path.

But I had other plans. I wanted something of MY OWN, and I went after it.

My business continues to grow, along with my employees. This number has varied. Currently, there are two other people in my company besides me (two full-time, one part-time). Over the years, I have also had success with college interns as well as a "virtual" employee. Because I work from my home and set my own hours, my "virtual" employee is fantastic. We correspond via e-mail, and he does his work from his own home with his own computer. It is a fabulous relationship and has created more time for me to spend on marketing.

My home office has had numerous locations! When I first started my business, I had a smaller apartment, so my office was in my bedroom (BIG mistake, by the way!). Now that I have moved into my own house, I have a separate room for my office. The space is similar to a den and has several windows and a sliding door leading to a deck. The sense of open space and the outdoors really help me focus and provide a great atmosphere for work.

Her greatest obstacles?

The toughest part of running my business is trying to accomplish so much in a given day. Sometimes I wish I could clone myself, so there would be 10 of me working.

I also struggle with administration. I'm creative—NOT organized! Running a business involves more than making the decision to start selling a product or service online, and I definitely struggle with keeping my affairs in working order.

Without a doubt, the best part of my business is that it is HOME-BASED meaning that I can operate it from anywhere as long as I have a computer and Internet access.

Just one week ago, I returned home to Rhode Island from six glorious months in sunny south Florida! I'm 27 years old, and I am already able to spend summers in New England and winters in Florida.

I have been asked many times what I "least" like about my business or if I could go back in time, what would I change? My answer is always the same. I would eliminate those periods of isolation. I was so eager to make my business work and so desperate for it to start making money at the beginning, that I made the commitment in my mind to throw myself into it. From the very beginning, I immersed myself into a 16-hour-a-day, seven-day-a-week mission. I resigned myself to the fact that if I was awake, I was going to be working. This was absolutely the biggest mistake that I made throughout the operation of my first home-based Internet business. I believe that my earnings and productivity were diminished as a result.

My advice: Separate your "home-office" from your "home"— and set strict working hours. Also, in life, there is time for work and play!

What's next on the horizon for her business?

I'm a firm believer in diversity. Have a series of different home-based Internet businesses. Your first product and your first business are just the beginning. I already have a series of businesses that I operate online, but I want to continue to add to that. I absolutely love the creation process involved in started a new business. I love to put the Web site together and officially launch each new venture.

On a personal note, soon I will be ready to start a family, and I am grateful for my lifestyle. I see the benefits that working from home will bring when I have children.

What advice does she have for others?

Go for it! Let nothing stop you.

An Internet business that you work from home can be an outlet for self-expression. It can lead you toward contentment, confidence, and self-worth—things even more important than the almighty dollar. A successful home-based business can also go a long way toward eliminating the stress of making ends meet and having the luxury of free time. I'm living proof that it works, and that it is possible.

If you believe in yourself and you have the work ethic and determination to follow through no matter what happens, you can be telling your own success story soon.

How does she use Idea Cafe to help her business?

Sometimes I sit at home staring at my computer and think I'm all alone. It's so nice to be able to come to a place like Idea Cafe and hear from others who are doing the same thing! It's a great motivating source. I love to read the profiles. With everything in life I tend to learn from example. I do my research, see what the successful people are doing, and learn from them. I'm a firm believer in surrounding myself with the thoughts, ideas, and concepts of people who are making it happen!

Watson-Knobel Publishing Company

Name: Stephanie Watson

Name of company: Watson-Knobel Publishing Company

Location: Huntsville, AL

Web site: www.wahcornucopia.com

Type of business: Author, Home-Business Consultant, Web Site Designer & Internet MarketerOnline marketing for offline businesses locally

I started doing business online in 1998. Then I went back to college, received my business degree in 2005, and now I am back with a vengeance. My current Web site offers Internet tools and business tips to businesses, and my planned Ezine is coming soon! I will be earning double my current work outside of home job income within the next two years and will be able to devote myself full-time to my own business. Currently, my office is in my bedroom. Soon I will have a bigger house with a "real" office, but it will be in my home. I don't want a big office some place; the whole purpose for an online business is to work from home.

I plan to expand my publishing company to put out a magazine locally as well as on the Web promoting local interests. I also have a general work-at-home site that is designed to provide tools (that have worked for me) to others online entrepreneurs. I am working on brand new Web sites (yes, that is plural), working on the offline aspects of the magazine, layout, logo, and writing. I hope to launch the print magazine in January 2007. The Web-based Ezine is set for mid-year 2006!

My biggest obstacle has been my belief in ME. The hardest part has been both getting others to believe in me and getting myself to believe in me too. Funding is also one of the most difficult aspects of an online business but as my capital grows, so does my belief in my own abilities.

Her advice for new entrepreneurs?

I would have moved a lot faster. I am the type who wants to research and learn every aspect of something before I start whatever it is, and sometimes my self-education can get in the way of action. Education is great, but DOING IT is what gets you there.

I know it sounds trite, but believe in yourself, and you really can do anything you set your mind to.

CHAPTER 3

Merchandise and Retail

SUCCESS STORIES

The merchandise and retail section serves as a guide for creating, growing, and even pairing dual operations. You may find that one area complements, not competes with the other area.

Your retail customer may also like to refer to your online information, or once you sell to an online customer, he or she may want to visit your retail location. Either way, these Success Stories are proof that the pairing of resources can produce phenomenal success!

Rory McLoughney

Name: Rory McLoughney
Name of company: RPM Sports—The Powerball People!
Web site: www.powerballs.com

We ran a busy "bricks and mortar" cellular phone operation in my hometown during the nineties. In 1997 I hopped on a plane and headed for Asia to see if we could locate some other products, which would run alongside this core business. I picked up two good products—the first a high GSM booster unit and the second, our beloved Powerball.

Shortly after I got home, I bought copies of Dreamweaver and Fireworks then started creating sites for both products in an attempt to give them some online exposure.

The first site we created for Powerball was truly cringe-worthy; it never ceases to amaze me that we received an order for it.

The second incarnation was a little better, and sales began to increase. We were now managing at least four or five sales each week! Miserable numbers for sure, but in fairness, we didn't know how to market the site and only generated 60 or 70 visitors a week. At least we knew that the product had good market appeal given the relatively high conversion ratio.

Since then it is fair to say that there have been about two or three redesigns of Powerballs.com to bring us to the current site design. Each redesign has brought in some vital new element which was lacking in the previous version helping to boost sales and visitor numbers. I still design and build the sites because I know the product so well at this stage. I can relay this knowledge accurately in the site content.

Even though we are located in a small town in the very heart of the Irish countryside, we have successfully managed to launch our splendid spheres into virtually every corner of the globe to a greatly valued customer base comprising of sports enthusiasts, fitness enthusiasts, gadget lovers, and people undergoing wrist/arm reha- bilitation. That's a pretty wide net from an otherwise small boat.

The key elements of success and their advice to startups would be to find a need, find a product to fill it, and be persistent. Apart from having a white-hot product like Powerball, the single biggest factor for success in an online business is outright focus on total customer satisfaction.

You could have the very best product in the world, but if you can't deliver a quality customer experience from the onset through the sale then you'll crash and burn very quickly. We started small and have adopted this attitude right from the beginning. As a result, it helped us develop a solid customer base on which to build a fast-growing business. Each inquiry, no matter how small or trivial, gets a personalized response. While this takes time each week, the result is huge positive feedback and repeat business from our existing customers who recommend us to their friends. You need only look at the testimonial page on the site to see what our customers really think of this personalized service.

Of course, we do mess up from time to time also particularly with the introduction of SPAM filters to try to cull the thousands of SPAM mails that arrive each day. Sometimes our customers' e-mails get included with these and aren't spotted in a timely fashion, but when this happens we hold our hands up quickly and do what it takes to address the matter. Never lose sight of the customer, regardless of your level of success.

Hoffman Marketing

Names: Brad and Deb Hoffman
Web site: www.budtoblooms.com
Associate company: www.filter4life.com
E-mail: bnhoffman@pa.net

Brad Hoffman has a degree in Business Administration/ Accounting and worked as an assistant controller of a large corporation from 1974 until 1985, and then as VP/Controller of a small company from 1985 until 1993. At that point, Brad decided business ownership was his next move. His wife, Deb, had worked in retail sales, as a bank teller, a bookkeeper and secretary, and also had a candy and greeting card vending route.

In 1993, Brad and Deb started their own business, Clear Solutions of PA, and have continued to grow and branch into other areas. In 2003, they attended a SOL Business Seminar and purchased six Web site hosting packages. Brad said, "We then selected our products, found our suppliers, and started building our sites."

In July 2003 they launched their Web sites and started their PPC advertising program. They made $500 in sales their first month, and sales have been increasing ever since. Current BudtoBlooms.com sales average $460 per day with YTD sales of $63,000. They recently received a contract for an order totaling $12,260.

Their motivation for building their own business was to gain control of their time and income. The ultimate goal was to be able to work and travel simultaneously.

Their first products were silk flowers, plants, and trees. It is still one of their most successful Web sites.

The biggest obstacle for Brad and Deb was to learn how to use their site building software and then to begin routing traffic to their Web sites. Thanks to hard work, persistence, and experimentation, they have experienced the success that is the American dream!

Their advice to would-be entrepreneurs? Choose your products and suppliers wisely, know your competition, and be persistent.

McGroarty Enterprises, Inc.

Name: Mike McGroarty
Web site: www.freeplants.com
Associate company: www.learnfrommike.com

Mike began his online business in 1999 with 30 plus years of landscaping and nursery experience. In 1985 he became very interested in marketing and mail order marketing.

> *When the Internet came along I applied what I had learned about mail order to the Internet. I never realized much success in mail order, but eventually became very good at Internet marketing. I first published a small paperback book on gardening (plant propagation) and decided to try to sell my book online. I knew little about computers, nothing about Web page design, and nothing about how to attract visitors to my Web site. So today when I check my stats and see that 260 people joined my mailing list in a single day, I'm still dumbfounded.*

Mike's motivating factor was the national appeal of marketing his product versus marketing it locally.

His first product sold online was his paperback gardening book. It was priced at $9.97 plus $2.00 shipping and handling. In the first 30 days, he didn't sell a single copy, but after the 34th day, he had sold 3 copies. That was just enough to break even on the cost of the Web site. After that, the business continued to grow, and when he tallied up last month, he had sold over $27,000 in information products in just 30 days. Mike said it boggles the mind, since it wasn't that long ago he was hoping for the next $11.95 order.

The biggest obstacle Mike faced when launching his own business was his lack of knowledge about the Internet and the marketing tools he would need. He had no knowledge of computers, or how he could create a Web page from his living room that other people would be able to view on their home computer, no matter where their location. Mike said, "My lack of knowledge was extremely intimidating. In fact, when I first purchased Web design software, I returned the software to the store, unopened before the expiration of the return policy. Two months and much debate later, I returned to the store, purchased the Web design software along with two 'how to' books, and in a few short weeks, uploaded my Web page to the Internet."

We asked him about the personal characteristics that led to success. He said sheer determination, persistence, and the willingness to seek out the information he needed to succeed.

The more I read about selling information the more I realized the potential for success. I had a willingness to work hard at something that wasn't guaranteed to work. You have to be willing to work without immediate reward, but if you understand the potential, you know that it's only a matter of finding the right combination. Don't expect it to work with your first, second, or even third attempt. Look at the potential reward and be realistic. If it were really easy, everyone would be an entrepreneur. Only those willing to make some sacrifice will succeed.

His advice to startup businesses?

Pay for the information you need to be successful. It's not necessary to have a college degree or spend thousand of dollars on educating yourself. If you expect to be successful, there are times you will need to purchase information or services to help you achieve your goals. Don't be afraid to invest in yourself and your goals. If it seems too good to be true, it probably is. Set and follow realistic goals; be persistent, patient, and willing to learn. It's the shortest path to success.

The Carolina Sauce Co.

Names: Gloria Cabada-Leman and Greg Leman

Date started: August 2003

Web site: www.carolinasauce.com

E-mail: sales@carolinasauce.com

Formerly an attorney at a software company and before that a partner at a law firm, Gloria Cabada-Leman has always had a passion for creating zesty foods and hot sauces. After the software company she was working for closed in the spring of 2003, Gloria and her husband, Greg Leman, spend the summer researching the specialty foods industry and online stores. In August 2003, Carolina Sauce Company, Inc., and **www.carolinasauce.com** were born. The company has distinguished itself from competing "hot sauce" Web sites by offering the most comprehensive selection of North Carolina sauces (including BBQ sauces, hot sauces, jerks, dry rubs, and spicy snacks made in North Carolina) on the Internet, and providing superb customer service with a personal touch. The unifying theme for the over 300 different products offered at Carolina Sauce is zesty flavor. While many of the products are hot and spicy, the Web site also offers mild (non-peppery) products that nevertheless offer bold, zesty flavors.

During the interview, we asked Gloria how she began her online business.

Greg Leman, co-founder and resident "tech guru," researched the technical requirements for launching an online store. After a lot of research, hard work, and personal investment, he and Gloria launched the online store in 2003.

While Greg could be considered a "serial entrepreneur," having started and sold several software companies since his college days, Gloria had always been the "conservative" or risk-averse one, preferring the relative safety of a large law firm or corporate practice. After 9/11 and the end of the dot-com boom, Gloria decided it was time to follow a dream she had since 1997, when Greg was working for a software company in CA while Gloria practiced law in North Carolina. Back then, the plan was for Gloria to move to California to join Greg and start her own online specialty foods store. However, when Greg resigned from the company in California to start yet another software company in North Carolina, Gloria's dream was put on hold. But when the opportunity came up again in 2003, she jumped on it.

Their first successful online product began with several different North Carolina BBQ sauces that are otherwise only available in regional stores in North Carolina. Transplanted North Carolinians were elated to be able to order their favorite sauces and have them shipped promptly to them, anywhere in the world!

The biggest obstacle faced, as with all startup businesses was a lack of financial resources to really advertise and market the business as well as I'd like to. If you simply build a Web site, people will not necessarily visit it. It takes a lot of hard work and resources to market your site and bring customers to it. You may be able to do it on a "shoestring," but the growth will be much slower.

When asked what made their business the success it is today, Gloria responded:

> *I am driven and passionate about what I do. I am willing to put in the long hours necessary to make my business successful, and I have learned to take risks and be flexible. That means being willing to drop an idea that turns out not to work and adjust as necessary. I am also familiar with the products I sell, and I am a highly*

organized "detail person." Finally, I strive to provide excellent customer service, responding to customer inquiries and concerns in a timely manner. I am always looking for new products while keeping an eye on the competition to make sure I stay ahead of the game

What advice does she have for other entrepreneurs?

Don't assume that all you need to do is build a Web site and customers will come. Do your homework: scope out the competition, assess whether you have the determination to work long hours, come up with a realistic budget, and pick something that you enjoy doing.

www.KozyKomfortbyKaren.com

Names: Gerald and Karen West

Name of the company: G K West Enterprise
Associate companies: www.fauxfurcomforters.com, www.kwestex.com, www.kozykomforbykaren.net, www.obviousintentions.com, www.gkwestenterprise.com

E-mail: kozykomfortbykaren@yahoo.com

Gerald and Karen West have 10 years experience in sales and business ownership. In September of 2003, they attended a StoresOnline Workshop that changed their lives. Prior to sales, Gerald had worked for 32 years as an owner/operator in the freight business. Retirement was drawing ever closer, and they needed supplemental income. This is their story.

In September of 2003, we went to a StoresOnline Workshop. We were interested in the possibility of supplementing our retirement which was about six years away. We were intrigued by what we heard at the workshop, and we thought we could do this part-time until our retirement. We purchased some store fronts from StoresOnline, and then we began our search for products to sell on our future Web sites. Once we made those choices, we started our journey of building Web sites and acquiring manufacturers. We now have seven different Web sites, and we are on Amazon.com shopping portal. We have more planned.

The motivation to begin our online business stemmed from the need to supplement our retirement income. I became legally blind due to retina detachments, and seven operations later I was forced into a medical retirement and needed a way to supplement that income. We knew that we could earn a living on the Internet with a lot of hard work and study. Since time was of the essence, we brought our son into work with us. He does the tech and background work, and we operate the business side of the work.

Our first product to sell was quilts, and we soon realized we needed to have a complete line of contemporary bedding for our customers. Business has continued to grow from there.

The biggest obstacle we faced when launching our business was our physical limitations, our age, and our lack of knowledge. We need to learn and retain information about operating a business on the Internet. Neither of us was knowledgeable about computers.

The personal elements to success in our situation were hard work, learning, staying focused, and persistence. In the near future, we plan to turn the business over to our children. This will give them long-term financial stability and an early retirement.

The best advice we have for someone starting a business today would be to stay focused, learn all you can every day, be persistent, and learn from your mistakes. Subscribe to a good online newsletter and make yourself familiar with SEO and search engines.

All American Watches

Name: James Lane

Web site: www.allamericanwatches.com

Associate companies: www.allamericanclocks.com, www.acornhomemortgage.com

E-mail: cjameslane@optonline.net

James Lane is very animated-and very entertaining. A native of the UK, Citigroup brought him to New York to work in banking. Then one day his Wall Street job dried up. He had never had any entrepreneurial experience before, but decided it was time for him to be in more control of his own life. At a StoresOnline presentation, he remembers the presenter saying, "The difference between those who dream of being in business and those who are in business is that those who are in business finally chose one day to start." That simple statement spurred him on.

"That speaker changed my life," James said. "I have friends who have dreamed of being in business 20 years. And they even laughed at me for trying what I'm doing. But there they are, still drawing a paycheck while I have three businesses online."

He got a flyer inviting him to the StoresOnline preview in May 2003. He went to the presentation at Stamford, Connecticut because of the proposition of making money on the Internet. He had seen enough people making money that he thought he'd like to get a piece of that, too. He basically made up his mind at the preview that he wanted an Internet business and went to the workshop with his checkbook in hand. He looks back on that day and laughs because the person next to him had an established, growing business with a strong mail-order base. And he didn't buy!

"That poor guy probably had more reason to sign up than

anybody and he didn't! James bought his Web sites after listening to the many marketing techniques presented at the workshop.

"I realized there are many more ways to market on the Internet than with just search engines," he said. "I was very impressed with the sound marketing principals taught by StoresOnline. They teach a strategy. And I haven't even used a fraction of the possibility of the options yet." He learned so much from the presentation and was so inspired by it that some day he'd like to come back and speak as a guest merchant to show people all the possibilities on the Internet.

Using the advice StoresOnline offered about choosing a product, he chose one that he loves — watches. "I did what they told me to," he said. "I brainstormed a list and then used the reverse search to see what interest there might be in those items. It was very sound teaching. I have so much information on that Web site that it has been linked to information.org sites."

He chose to specialize in selling Bulova watches — although they weren't the first product he examined. With true Wall Street zeal, James searched the yellow pages and made calls. Then he gave several presentations to watch companies, eventually settling on Bulova. Once his product choice was made, he began voraciously researching Bulova watches.

"We have become a hub for information on the Internet for specific topics. I researched Bulova's history and rerecorded it for them. I had to contact NASA to get the details of how they began. Their company reps had forgotten, or didn't know, most of the details of their origins!" he said incredulously.

Then he published his site. It took about a month to make his first sale. But it was when he implemented one of the marketing techniques taught at the StoresOnline workshops-pay-per-click advertising that traffic really began to flow. "If the first day I published, I had used this technique, I would have been selling from the first day. It's beautiful the way it works."

Since then, he has become quite adept at tailoring his marketing efforts. He has bid on over 600 items with the pay-per-click engines. He has also spent quite a bit of time getting his Web site to work correctly on the relativity search engines (his site ranks on over 450 search terms). He believes it is certainly worth his time to work with the relativity search engines because the number one place pulls even more than the number one spot on the sponsored listing.

During the whole process StoresOnline was there. "I received a lot of encouragement and help from StoresOnline to get the maximum benefit from the Web site. It's a new experience to learn how to promote a product," he said. "I'm very impressed with the whole game." And the future looks bright for James Lane.

He admits, though, that the first storefront is probably the toughest to get going. "You have to be totally enthusiastic to make it work." But overall, he calls launching an online business an easy endeavor.

"I'm not a very smart person," he said modestly. "But I do work hard. The competition clearly doesn't know what they are doing. There is no reason that 97 percent of Internet businesses shouldn't at least cover their hosting fees. But I think there's a reason. Most people believe in the old 'field of dreams' approach: If you build it they will come. Then if it doesn't get traffic, they don't spend the time to make it work. I don't think you have to be smart to do this. You just have to be focused and committed."

TK Better Business

Name: Tom Kress
Web site: www.theferipump.com
Associate company: www.tkbetterbusiness.com
E-mail: tom@tkbetterbusines.com

Tom Kress is the owner of TK Better Business which he started as a way to escape the hassles of a regular job.

I wanted a change of lifestyle and after looking and trying various things, I decided the Internet was the way to go. I now work the hours I want, can live where I want (I have a small ranch out in the country), and travel the world. I learned about building and running Web sites the hard way–by looking through the Net, talking to people, and finding the information I needed. Then I put it all together. This was very frustrating at times. Then Stores Online came along, and they had the complete package: everything I needed in one place. I found a product, and I'm now making my living on the Internet.

The greatest motivation for my Internet business stemmed from the fact that I was sick of regular jobs, set working hours, arrogant bosses and spending two weeks out of four away from home. I wanted flexibility to be able to work even when the travel bug bit me, which happens frequently. Otherwise, I just get up, feed the horses, walk the dog, work a little, and do what I want when I want.

The first product I sold continues to be the product I sell today: Feri submersible pumps. My biggest obstacle was simply getting started and developing my Web site.

What are her personal success secrets?

Determination, persistence, and dedication. For anyone interested in starting an online business, start small. Be prepared to learn many new things, be prepared for the odd failure, but keep at it. Occasionally stand back and look form the outside to see where you are going. Look at the big picture without being sidetracked by small things that occur. And last, find a mentor—someone to bounce ideas around with and to give you needed advice.

KABOOM!

Name: Tammy Hitzemann
Name of the company: KABOOM! Online Rock-n-Roll Shop
Date started: June 5, 2004
Web site: www.kaboomfla.com
E-mail: kaboomfla@yahoo.com

My name is Tammy Hitzemann and I am a 38-year-old married mother of two sons, Max and Sam. I am a former juvenile probation officer and before starting my own business, an eighth grade English teacher. I have a Bachelor of Science Degree in Criminology from Florida Gulf Coast University in Ft. Myers, Florida.

KABOOM! was the brain child of my eighth grade students. They came up with the idea of needing a youth-oriented business in our community. They helped with researching vendors and ultimately placing the first orders for the retail storefront.

In the two years of existence, KABOOM! has also been profiled in The St. Petersburg Times, *the* Business Owner's Idea Cafe, *an audio book (waiting for release) and in Stephanie Chandler's book,* The Business Startup Checklist and Planning Guide.

During my second year of teaching eighth grade English, I decided I needed a career change. I challenged my students to come up with businesses that they felt were lacking in our area. KABOOM!

was a result of my students' brainstorming. We originally opened KABOOM! as a brick-and-mortar store before turning to the Internet, full-time in June of 2005.

What motivated Tammy to begin her own business?

When I was teaching, I was controlled by students, their parents, administration, district administrators, and the Florida Department of Education's tests and regulations. At the same time I could see my small paychecks too! It didn't add up. All of these bosses, all of this hard work, and little money. I felt I had more creativity and energy than to continue working for someone else, but it really took teaching to make that more pronounced.

What was her first product?

An item on eBay. One day, in my brick-and-mortar store, I started looking at eBay. I had never really been around their site. I began researching the products that I was selling to see what they were going for on eBay. It consumed me for about two weeks before I tried my own auction.

I put one messenger bag, up for auction, on eBay. I spent seven days watching it like a hawk. I had done all the research I could before this auction, so I wanted to find out if I was right. Sure enough! The bag auctioned for 30 percent more than I could sell it in my storefront. That was it. I was hooked. I closed the storefront ,and we remodeled part of our house for my office and warehouse.

What was the biggest obstacle she had to face when she was launching her own business?

Money, money, money. I knew from all of my research that money was the key factor in starting my own business. I had the drive, the knowledge, and the emotional support, but I had to raise enough money to stay afloat.

The personal elements that brought Tammy to her present success?

I don't fear failing as much as I fear having to ever have a boss again. It keeps me motivated to continue to work hard and have future goals for the business. The days when I think, "A regular paycheck would be nice," I just remember all of my past bosses and work environments, and then I am back to business immediately!

What key advice would she have for someone starting an online business today?

Your business has to be something you know. Starting a business from the ground up is work enough, but if you try to learn a new trade or product, you would be tired and frustrated. I knew the rock 'n' roll apparel industry from watching my teenage students. I was aware of the hottest bands, styles of apparel, what accessories they would buy, and what they would avoid. I had hands-on research every day. So when it came to leave teaching and open the shop, I was ready.

Image

Name: Janet Dukes
Location: Sioux Falls, SD
Web site: www.imageleathers.com
Type of Business: Online Retail Stores

We own six Web sites. The first site we opened carries leather goods such as leather jackets/coats, purses/handbags, and luggage/ backpacks. Our second site is an online mall. In our mall, we have many stores that sell books, music, movies, concert tickets, clothing and accessories, jewelry, party supplies, kitchen accessories, bed/ bath accessories, office supplies, and pet supplies.

My partner, Maurice, and I started our online business since we both love working on the computer. Because of that, we felt this was a natural choice for us when it came to deciding what type of business to go into. Having our own business has been a dream of both of ours for as long as either of us can remember. Maurice had a concrete business a few years ago and knows what it's like to be his own boss. Once you know that feeling, it never leaves you, and nothing else can replace it! Our first site, **www.imageleathers. com** *was live in June 2005. Our second site,* **www.imagemall-lonline.com** *went live in September 2005. Hopefully, four more will go live very soon. At the moment, our office is located in a corner of our basement. Since starting our business we've accumulated a lot of paperwork, though, so we may need to expand our area so we can add a few filing cabinets. Since there are only the two of us, we manage with the limited space.*

What was their inspiration?

Both Maurice and I have always had the entrepreneurial "bug." I think between the two of us, it's inevitable that we would go into business. My daughter, Sarah, has been so supportive of all of my business ideas. All of her life, she's told people that her Mom would someday start a business and be successful with it. Now that Maurice and I have started our online business, I know between the two of us, we will be extremely successful with it. Thank you, Sarah, for always believing in me. Maurice and I will show you that belief was not in vain!

What was the most difficult part?

So far the toughest part is finding more time to devote to our business. We are both still working full-time, so we only have evenings and weekends to work on our Web sites. Learning about Web site design has also been difficult and slow. Every time we would get "stumped" on a Web site design or some other problem, we've learned the best thing is to not be afraid to ask someone who knows. Early on, we found ourselves trying to go it alone. We wasted a lot of time stressing over things when if we had just asked, we could have saved a lot of time and energy. Also, we found that we should have had more faith in our abilities. There were times we'd say, "We can't possibly learn how to do all of this!" when in reality, once we worked on it, things came so much easier to us. After a while, we felt more confident and realized that we could actually do it.

What's the most fun part?

It's so exciting to see something that starts out as an idea, actually turn into a live Web site! As we come up with ideas of how one of our Web sites should look and then seeing what we pictured actually happen, it is so exhilarating! Plus we really enjoy each other's company so this gives us something that we can work on together.

What's next on the horizon for her business?

We're always updating and making changes to our two "live" Web sites. This not only makes our sites better, but it keeps the information current. At the moment, we're also looking into several ideas for our other four Web sites. We're having so much fun at this business that we're hoping to have all six sites up and running as soon as possible. Eventually, we'd love to be able to do this full-time. That's the ultimate goal for our business.

When is her advice for others?

If you have a dream to own your own business, don't hold back. It's not unlikely that you'll have to start it while still working at your regular job, but don't let that stop you. Yes, you'll be tired and some days you won't have the slightest desire to look at your business after a hard day at work. But when those feelings come, just keep in mind how great it'll be once that business starts making enough money to allow you to do it full time! The satisfaction and pride you'll feel once that happens will make it all worthwhile. Also, don't forget: NEVER be afraid to ask for help.

There's a great Web site known as Idea Café that is really helpful. It's funny, but when I found Idea Café several years ago, my daughter always laughed at me whenever I would log on, because I'd get lost in cyberspace for hours. There is so much wonderful information to be found here, I would just lose track of time! It ended up that I'd have to "warn her" ahead of time before I'd log on. Otherwise, if she needed to do homework or wanted to check her e-mail, she'd have to wait a long time. One of my favorite things to look at is the "Businesses Profiles." They keep me sane in the knowledge that others have gone through what we've gone through while starting our business. I've received inspiration, advice, and so much knowledge from reading the profiles and other information found on Idea Café. Anyone who ever mentions to me that they'd like to open a business of their own, or those of my friends who already own one, I always send them to Idea Café. But I do warn them that they too will get lost for hours on this wonderful site!

Plain Brown Tabby Toes and Treats

Name: Patricia Krook, Owner	
Name of Company: Plain Brown Tabby Toys and Treats	
Date Started: September 9, 2002	
Web site: www.catniptoys.com	
E-mail: Information@catniptoys.com	

I earned a Bachelor of Arts degree from Hobart and William Smith College, intending to pursue a career in writing. Later I went back to school, earning an Associates Degree in nursing and becoming a registered nurse. During a 13-year career on a busy high-risk labor and delivery unit, I pursued a hobby of showing my cats. I became involved in promoting a very rare breed of cat, the American Curl for relaxation in my off-time.

Her online business began because of cats.

It developed out of my love for cats and my love of researching new toys, new treats, and finding classic cat toys no longer sold in the big super pet stores. I wanted to be the place where folks could find both the newest toys, treats, and the classic hard-to-find toys.

I have a plump, sassy-mouthed American Curl nicknamed Alix, and I used to "speak" for her on a cats' forum. I first decided it would be fun to have a cookbook by pets and to offer that for sale. That evolved into my deciding to begin my own business with an online storefront, where I could offer the toys and treats I prefer for my cats. I love researching, I love shopping, and I love creating cat gift baskets such as my Tabby Takeout and toys such as my Tabby Tuffet. It all came together into my business.

Her first product for success?

Kitty Kaviar! After receiving a sample of this treat when I began my business, I knew I had to offer it. It quickly became and remains my number one selling all natural cat treat.

Her biggest obstacle?

Belief in self. Believing that someone who never intended to be, never saw herself as a business owner, could be one. Second, starting without a loan, I wish I'd had more money at the beginning for products.

What personal elements contributed to her success?

Stubbornness, creativity, love of cats, and all things for cats, and faith. I believe I can meet the goals I set, and once I have, I set new ones.

Her advice for beginners:

- *Be passionate. Love what you are going to be selling or the service you will be providing. Since you will be thinking about this business 24/7, it better be something you are interested in!*

- *Research. Know what it is you will offer and why you want to offer it — how does it fit in with your concept of your business? What is your mission? What will distinguish you from every other online business in your field? Understand what is available in your area of business and become very knowledgeable about the products you will carry.*

- *Be focused. Do an initial detailed business plan regardless of whether you are applying for a loan. Use it as a tool to focus on what monthly expenses will be, what initial stock you need, what your monthly sales goals are for your first year.*

- *Define your target audience and how you will reach them to introduce yourself to them. Update this business plan every year or as needed.*

CHAPTER

4

Distributors and B2B

SUCCESS STORIES

Perhaps this last section covers the areas that are still most open to exploration and innovation. Distributorships and B2B business services are experiencing tremendous growth, as more and more businesses outsource, globalize, and customize. Never before has the world been at your doorstep more than it is with this current business opportunity. Businesses can reach across the globe to do business with different governments, cultures, and organizations. As the increased business opportunities create more work, more of the workload is being shifted to the "expertise" or "customized" market niche. Here's a frontier still vastly unexplored and inhabited. And here's your big chance!

JPE Advertising

Name: Jane Mark & Phil Basten

Date started: 2001

Web site: www.jpeadvertising.com

Type of business: JPE Advertising is an online ad agency

The principals, Jane Mark and Phil Basten, star in the Internet's first radio "soap opera" on the Internet marketing called *Joe? Yes Mable? Are We Rich Yet?* at **wwwjoeandmable.com**.

> *Our secret to success: dogged persistence to overcome any challenge and being able to laugh at ourselves when we don't quite make it.*

Jane Mark has a Masters degree in psychology, and Phil Basten has a diploma in professional counseling. The opportunity to work in a situation that allows for optimal creativity and customer service is the foundation for their continued success. Jane told us:

> *We love the ebb and flow of our business. I am an early riser and run to the computer at 4 a.m. to see what orders came in, who needs help, and to work on another "Joe and Mable" episode. Phil works late hours into the night perfecting new Web sites or talking to our programmers in Russia and England and our partners all over the world. We simply love what we do, and we are eager to create whatever is around the next corner. In some ways that's contagious. People sense that we know what we are doing and that we believe in the products we offer, and they respond to that. The Joe and Mable Show, which has given people a good laugh and is great fun for us to do, has given us a terrific name on the Web (or maybe it's notoriety). Whatever it is, it seems to work for us.*

What advice do they have for the budding entrepreneur?

> *Read about the product or service you intend to sell. After you do your research on what you want to sell, you must get your hands on every effective marketing book you can find. Many of them are free, and you can do a search on Google to find books and reports related to your particular business.*
>
> *Next, make sure you hire a great Web designer and copywriter who can give you not just a Web site but a sales site so that*

when you begin to advertise, you have something that will capture people's attention This is essential if you want to succeed on the 'Net.

Next, start a list. Start an Ezine so you can grow your list over time. You must have an opt-in list where you can e-mail your contacts. Nurture and grow your list so that you can continually communicate with your clients, develop a relationship of trust with them, and they will buy from you when you recommend a product.

Most important, never fail and never give up. We've hit some rough points over the three years we have been in business. There were times when we didn't know if we would make it through some of the months when we had to choose between food or paying the server bill. The server bill always won out. We refused to quit—ever—and we think that's the attitude you must have in any business.

Before the interview, Jane and Phil had just spoken with someone interested in a start-up business. The caller's husband had just given her a six-month window of opportunity to succeed or give it up. We asked for their reaction.

We said: tell your husband six months is not enough time to develop a successful business. Most businesses need at least a year (if you are lucky) and, more likely, two years to develop to the point where they can be called "a living." For the first six months, you should be putting back into your business any profits you realize so you can continue to grow. You will also need to put aside money for emergencies, refunds, legal advice, advertising, sales copy, conferences, and continuing education. Six months is too short a trigger. Tell your husband to have some patience—a limited vision does not a good business plan make.

As for the question of start-up capital, small business loans, or private funding, Jane and Phil were explicit.

> *Whenever you start a business, you need to ask yourself some pointed questions. Do you have the persistence to keep going when times get tough—and they will? Are you comfortable using OPM (other people's money)? If so, by all means take out a loan. However, if you are just dabbling and don't know if you will see your new business through, it is best to save and use your own capital. You will sleep better at night.*

Do they feel that success has changed them or their perspective, and what were their personal objectives?

> *We haven't really changed since we've had success. We are proud of our business and our reputation, but we never went into our business to own mansions or a yacht. Mostly, we just wanted an outlet and a business that would let us use our talents, and JPE Advertising has provided that for us. Of course, we are in a unique position. If we don't like who we are at any one moment, we just change characters and become Joe and Mable, make each other laugh, and go on from there.*

> *We both have children and grandchildren whom we adore. We hope that they will look up to our success and strive to attain it for themselves in their own fields of interest. If we accomplish that, it will be a great blessing.*

Mailworkz

	Name: Julie MacLean, Marketing
	Name of company: MailWorkZ Inc.
	Date started: 1999
	Address: 1 Research Drive Dartmouth, Nova Scotia, B2Y 4M9
	Phone: 902-835-8975
	Web site: www.mailworkz.com
	E-mail: sales@mailworkz.com julie.maclean@mailworkz.com

MailWorkZ is a privately owned company founded in 1999. Our flagship product, Broadc@st e-mail marketing software, enabled us to become a leading provider of e-mail marketing software to all sizes of enterprises very quickly. Over the past few years we have added complementary products that our clients use to manage and control all aspects of their e-marketing campaigns. We will soon release a new Web-based e-mail marketing service.

Their online success is attributable to the e-mail marketing software they developed and sold online through our Web site.

The e-mail marketing software was the result of filling a market need. It was an innovative idea, and we saw an opening in the marketplace.

Their biggest obstacle was reaching the desired target market. The Internet is a door to a large marketplace, but a main obstacle was trying to target the right leads. Learning to find unique marketing venues and valuable means of advertising to our customers were challenges initially.

What advice do they have for startups today?

Start an opt-in e-mail list of your customers or contacts and have a method to manage and maintain that database.

Declan Dunn

Declan Dunn is CEO of AD'Net International, Web site **www. adnetinternational.com,** a direct marketing services provider that focuses on select projects and its own super affiliate network, including the 'Net Profits business training systems delivered at Active Marketplace, **www.activemarketplace.com.**

Declan has made his living with affiliate programs, and he has invented some of the affiliate programs we see on the 'Net today. He is a consultant and advisor in the area of affiliate systems to some of the biggest businesses in the industry.

He was one of the original Internet marketing gurus who pioneered affiliate marketing as we know it today. He writes from both the perspective of the small business person signing up with affiliate or associate programs, and he also instructs providers of the programs. So he reaches two completely separate markets with his lessons; both the little guy at home and the corporate giants alike are benefiting from his instruction.

He also speaks at seminars and public speaking events; he has spoken on countless radio shows as well as making appearances at major conferences and seminars with a focus on affiliate marketing.

His eBooks, *Winning the Affiliate Game* and *The Complete Insider's Guide to Associate & Affiliate Programs,* have become the textbook standard for the affiliate marketing industry. His products include *Winning The Affiliate Game: The Ten-Step Master Plan for Maximizing Your Profits, The Complete Insider's Guide to Associate &*

Affiliate Programs, and *'Net Profits: How to Win the Internet Game.*

Below he interviews Paul Colligan of FrontPage fame:

Article By Declan Dunn
January 2002

Most affiliate networks think affiliates are completely dependent on them. They are dead wrong. Smart affiliates know the game and adapt, becoming hybrid affiliates who sell their own products as well as products for others. Paul Colligan decided that if the affiliate programs weren't going to treat him right, he'd just become the merchant. It isn't that hard. It took him two weeks.

Paul runs a number of Web sites related to Microsoft FrontPage. Until recently, he generated 100 percent of his site revenue through affiliate programs. He has switched over to the other side: he is now a merchant. Not only does Paul make more money, but other affiliate programs will likely make more money, too. Here's why:

Smart affiliates figure out that to run a long-term business, you need to have customers loyal to you. If they buy from you and you treat them right, they will likely buy from you again.

Smart affiliates become resellers of their own products. If you don't sell people something, you can't build loyalty. Affiliates who only sell other products have trouble unless they have a huge e-mail list or loyal daily visitors.

Smart affiliates know that to thrive, they have to own a product or service to complement the affiliate programs they offer. The change intrigues me. Being both a merchant and an affiliate is smart because you acquire customers yourself—not just for others. In a sense, everyone is an affiliate and everyone is a merchant with a bigger pool of customers to endorse. Paul is taking that next step right now, and his income is likely to increase dramatically.

Here's a transcript of a conversation between us:

DUNN: *You began with a site,* ***www.frontpageworld.com****, which is driven by affiliate income. How is that different from* ***www.frontpagetools.com****?*

COLLIGAN: *FrontPageWorld.com was, and still is, an online resource for building business Web sites with FrontPage. It has information and tips, drawing people to look at and possibly buy affiliate products.* ***FrontPageTools.com*** *is a new site that targets small businesses. Everything can be downloaded immediately after purchase. I've added many of my own products, including templates and training. Being an affiliate inspired me to go to the next step—being a merchant.*

DUNN: *You removed your affiliate links and started selling your own product instead?*

COLLIGAN: *They aren't all gone. There are a few key ones where they should be. Heck, I still link to your stuff, and you still send me checks. It just isn't the focus anymore.*

DUNN: *If you were seeing good money from your affiliate relationships, why reinvent the wheel?*

COLLIGAN: *Well, first of all, it isn't as hard as a lot of people like to make it. I built the whole thing in a few weeks. It is really not rocket science anymore. The first reason was confusion. People wanted to know where I ended and where the other guy began—a common affiliate problem. People wanted to know whom to e-mail if there were problems. People wanted to know where the buck stopped. And, unfortunately, it stopped in a number of different places. In addition to this problem, my affiliate partners, and they were all great people, simply didn't have the infrastructure or desire to include me in the process as much as I felt I needed to be included. I'd get e-mails saying that "Joe" bought product "X," but I'd get no* *information on Joe's e-mail address or whether he liked the product. I'm not trying to violate privacy policies. I'm just trying to run a business, and many times I answered questions better than the merchant did! Obviously, the value of my bringing Joe to company "X" was always a subject for debate—but I'm sure that issue isn't unique to my situation. If a few people upped my commission and shared information with me so I could help the customers I sent them,* **FrontPageTools.com** *would have remained the batch of affiliate links it was 100 days ago.*

DUNN: I don't care how fast you build them, e-commerce sites are a lot of work. Is it worth it?

COLLIGAN: After you subtract all of the costs associated with **FrontPageTools.com**, *I'm making twice what I was making before—and the site is only 100 days old. I also now own the relationships. I own the names; I own the e-mail address; I own it all. That is where the value is. Over a month ago, I sent out a mailing to everyone who had previously purchased from me updating them about what was new at the site and, get this, 5 percent of them bought something else. That's a 5 percent conversion rate. I never had that before. I did it again, just to see if it was a fluke, and guess what—6.5 percent bought. And that list keeps growing—fast! In the short time the site has been up, I have been writing myself a check for three times as much as the affiliates ever did. And I own the names and contact information. This is a win/win situation for me. I'm adding about 500 names a month to the database. With a 5 percent conversion rate after 12 months and an average ticket price of $25, I should see $7,500 in sales every time I do a mailing. I like those numbers. Who wouldn't?*

DUNN: So, what next?

COLLIGAN: I've got some really interesting information on what sells well and what doesn't and, more important, why. I'll be putting that data to good use. I also am going to streamline the support process and make sure the customers are being as well served as possible. We also might hire someone to run the day-to-day stuff. I have some other things unrelated to FrontPage in the hopper. This should help pay for their development.

DUNN: What would you say you've learned from this process?

COLLIGAN: Honestly, if a few key affiliate programs had treated me just slightly better, they'd be getting some great business that they are no longer getting. It is that simple. It wasn't that they were purposely deceiving me or trying to keep me out of the loop—the issue is that they simply didn't have the infrastructure to keep me happy. And now I'm gone. And I'll bet I'm not the only one to go. I won't make the same mistakes with my affiliates.

DUNN: This is part of a new trend, the hybrid affiliate, part affiliate and part merchant. Watch for these folks rising up out of the early days of affiliate programs.

Declan's and Paul's successes resulted from addressing a need. Affiliate marketing is how many are introduced to the world of online business. When they first began, very few people really knew what to do to make real money.

Declan's information books are easy to understand and appeal to two large and growing online markets—both the beginners and the corporate giants.

He expanded his expertise into seminars and public speaking events to add another stream of income to his business. He used his writing talents and experience to make money with hot products—informational eBooks.

Politis Communications

Name of company: Politis Communications
Address: 65 E. Wadsworth Park. Dr., Suite 102 Draper, UT 84020
Web site: www.politis.com
E-mail: info@politis.com

David Politis is an award-winning public relations, investor relations and marketing communications professional, with **more than 50 industry awards** to his credit during his 19-plus years as a communications consultant.

Since his return to Utah in the fall of 1987, David has been involved in helping organizations throughout the United States and overseas succeed through aggressive public relations, investor relations, and marketing communications programs. These efforts have helped his clients generate increased visibility in the marketplace, grow sales and revenues, and raise stock market valuations on Wall Street.

He presently heads Politis Communications, an agency that specializes in working with organizations in the high-tech and life sciences industries, while also serving non-technical firms. Formed in 1990, Politis Communications was selected in 1999 by the **MountainWest Venture Group** (MWVG) as one of the 100 fastest growing firms in Utah as a member of the Utah100.

He has this advice for the 'netpreneur.

- *When looking for an outside consulting firm–and more specifically, a public relations or investor relations agency–the most important consideration is understanding what sets one organization apart from its competitors. From our perspective, there are five traits that help make Politis Communications unique.*

- *We're not order takers. If an organization is looking for an agency to do everything it's told without asking questions or looking for the better course of action (if one exists), we're the wrong agency. Another way of putting this is that we're not full of yes-men and yes-women.*

- *We're not public relations snobs. Many agencies only do PR; others only do advertising. We recognize that delivering the goods for our clients comes down to getting the right message to the right prospects at the right time. In some cases, that may mean getting some college students to parade around in gorilla suits while holding placards. If that's what it takes, so be it!*

- *We speak geek and plain English. Understanding technical jargon is a skill, and it's something we do quite well. Being able to translate geek-speak into customer benefits in plain English is something we do for our clients every day.*

- *We have the contacts. With an active database of more than 450,000 U.S.-based editors and industry analysts at our fingertips, we are well prepared to identify the best contacts for each of our clients. This database includes business and financial media, trade publications, television, radio and cable stations, newspapers and regional publications, syndicated columnists and reviewers, online publishers, and market research firms. In many instances, we know precisely how each individual prefers to be approached.*

- *We understand "Exit Strategies" and how to build "Shareholder Value." Since the formation of Politis*

Communications in 1990, agency representatives have been deeply involved in organizations such as the MountainWest Venture Group, T2M (Technology-to-Market), and the Utah Valley Entrepreneurial Forum while also serving as counsel to public companies and private companies raising risk capital. As a result, Politis Communications' professionals are profoundly aware of the need to increase shareholder value for firms before raising venture capital, going public, or pursuing an M&A plan. If your firm has an aggressive exit strategy and needs to maximize its perceived value, you must map your PR and marketing plans accordingly.

- *We understand and support this philosophy. Selecting an agency to support your company's communications objectives is never a fun job. However, we are confident that we have the experience and expertise to help you meet and exceed your goals.*

Adrian Ghoic

Runs a successful Ad Co-op, **www.adsmarket.business**.

AdsMarket.business is an ideal place for advertisers. You really must visit this site. Classified, top sponsor, and solo ads at low prices are just some of the goodies waiting for the savvy marketer. Adrian began his online success by publishing the Ezine *Home of Money Makers,* starting on January 17, 2001. Today, his ad co-op's success is due to the AdsMarket package which includes various types of advertisements published by his team of publishers.

What are the key elements to his success?

- *Providing prompt customer support.*

- *Continuous improvement of the quality of the service provided.*

- *Analyzing other businesses activities that sold similar products on a weekly basis.*

What is his advice for online startups today?

Be yourself but look around you at how others are doing business, be honest with your customers, make your own rules, and be the first to always comply with your rules.

Prosperity Coaching, LLC

Name: Suzanne Muusers

Location: Scottsdale, AZ

Phone: 902-835-8975

Phone: 480-922-1723

Web site: www. prosperitycoaching.business

Type of Business: Start-Up Business Coaching

At Prosperity Coaching, LLC We partner with entrepreneurs to build financial prosperity. Before starting the business in January 2004, I had started or managed five businesses over 25 years and was often asked to assist friends and family start their businesses. With my experience in retail ownership and management, international buying, accounting projects, and project management in the financial services field, I felt that I could succeed in the coaching business. Realizing that helping others become entrepreneurs was my calling in life, I took my professional coach training and started a business where I could realize my passion.

We are starting a group coaching experience for new entrepreneurial women in business three years or less: "Women Seeking Success," in the Scottsdale, Arizona area.

Our offices are virtual! The coaches maintain their own individual space, usually a home office, and assist clients through telephone or in-person coaching. My office has a view of a 30-year old pine tree. My pets Sunny, Emma, and Roca often hang around in case they are needed.

The most difficult aspect of coaching occurs when you have a clients who are completely overwhelmed with business. You feel their pain, but you just have to assure them that it will get better. Coaching is a process and results over time are a by-product of the process.

What is the motivation behind the business?

It's celebrating successes with clients, getting an e-mail or phone call with great news! Just today we received an e-mail from a client whose sales were up 104 percent over January of 2005. His enthusiasm was evident in the tone of the e-mail. This is what it's all about. This is why I started my business. Although there are some tough obstacles, most coaches we know wouldn't change a thing. Nothing. Everything in our lives happens for a reason. All these experiences have made us who we are and have contributed to our ability to help individuals who want to realize their dreams by having a profitable, successful business.

What advice do you have for others?

Get the help you need! Whether it's a trusted friend, mentor, family member, or a professionally-trained business coach, it's important to have structure and someone to hold you accountable for each goal you strive to attain.

Creative Answers

Name of company: Creative Answers
Location: Vancouver, British Columbia, Canada
Web site: www.creativeanswers.com
E-mail: carolann@creativeanswers.com
Type of Business: Business consulting

Basically I'm in the business of solving problems! Whether it's computer-related or simply functional, I have a knack for finding the answers. Prior to starting my own business I was Senior Vice President of Operations for Copelco Capital Corporation, Pennsauken, New Jersey. My field of expertise is equipment leasing; however, I have consulted and designed Web pages for a glass bead importer as well as a medical supply company. If you have a great idea, but you don't have time to put it in place, why not give me a call?

I started my company in 1995 when I retired from the corporate world. While I built the business, I got my graduate degree in elementary education, something I had dreamed of doing for a long time. I enjoy the flexibility of working for myself and can't think of a better way to spend the "second half of my life."

I have a small 10' x 10' room in the front of my house with a HUGE window facing my lovely front gardens. The room is cozy with two computer desks, a lateral filing cabinet, and a unit for supplies. Since there's only me, one room is large enough.

I'm an operating person all the way so the toughest part of running my business is doing the marketing. I have a tendency to sell myself short. The most fun part of my business is working in my pajamas until six at night and the satisfaction derived from completing a project for a satisfied customer.

When asked if there is anything she would have done differently, she said, "Not so far—even the mistakes have had their benefits."

My first successful product was the creative answers I've provided for my clients. However, I'm interested in the phenomenon of e-learning centers and would love to find the funds to experiment with creating one. I'm working on design and implementation of e-learning facilities.

What advice do you have for others?

Be ready for some lean years and always, always, always stay optimistic about the future.

VendorCentralUSA

Name Caryn FitzGerald
Date started: January 2004
Web site: www.VendorCentralUSA.com
Associate companies: www.VCUSAChapters.com
E-mail: caryn@vendorcentralusa.com

Caryn FitzGerald has a Masters of Professional Studies in Human Relations and 15 years experience in direct sales and marketing. She has provided mediation and counseling as a licensed therapist. Her online business began strictly by accident.

I was helping friends build their businesses after they had seen the results I had achieved. They were accessible only online so I ended up putting their information online for them. Before I knew it I had others contacting me, and I found that putting it all into one location simplified the situation. I began charging and my online business was born.

My motivation was a personal objective. I wanted to be home with my child and needed to replace my income. I did so and wanted to share my methods with others.

What was the first product that was successful?

Chapter memberships. We have chapters across the country; each chapter has individual memberships available to those in business for themselves. Once the memberships were offered, more people became involved building their businesses and networking with other serious business owners.

What has been her biggest obstacle?

Time. There are days when I don't have enough hours to complete what needs to be done. Another obstacle is that there are times when people don't view an independent woman in business as a serious business person. I have learned how to overcome this obstacle and now teach others how to do the same.

What is her formula for success?

I am outgoing and personable. My goal is to help others, and I try hard to make sure that shows through in everything I do. Being organized and disciplined also helps.

Her advice for new businesses?

First, make sure you are getting into something you truly love. Make sure to have a support system and people you can count on to help you through the rough days. Get as much as you can in order before you open your doors. Develop your business plan and talk with a local small business mentor to find out more about what is needed in your area.

MarketingForSuccess.com

Name of the company: MarketingForSuccess.com (Owned by In Mind Communications, LLC)

Date started: 1984

Web site: www.MarketingforSuccess.com
www.MarketingforSuccessStore.com

Associate companies: www.15secondmarketing.com

E-mail: ccook@marketingforsuccess.com

How did Charlie Cook become a marketing guru, an expert in helping people attract more clients online and offline to increase sales and profits? The manuals, coaching, and other marketing services Charlie provides are all based on one simple business concept: the purpose of marketing is to help your prospects get what they want and bring in more business.

Why use this small business marketing approach?

When you focus your marketing on helping your prospects rather than focusing on selling, you'll close more sales—a lot more sales!

Over the years Charlie has researched and tested a set of marketing principles, a marketing strategy, and a way of attracting clients and growing both their and his businesses; the result: a marketing methodology that can help you pull in a steady stream of clients and profits.

Charlie has been developing and perfecting this system for more than 20 years. He has written a half dozen marketing manuals and provides marketing mentoring to individuals and corporations so they can skip his long learning curve and go right to increasing their sales.

Charlie has provided marketing and management consulting

services to Fortune 500 companies that include AETNA, AT&T, Cendant, GTE, and Pitney Bowes as well as mid-sized companies like Citizens Utilities and Hartford Steam Boiler, and he has contributed to *Fortune, Hemispheres,* and *Forbes.* Thousands of copies of Charlie's training manuals have been bought and used by executives, managers, and trainers at hundreds of Fortune 500 companies including AT&T, Merck, Chevron, IBM, and Boeing as well as by marketing professionals, individuals, and entrepreneurs.

Charlie's marketing articles and marketing strategies have been widely published both online and in print. He's a regular columnist for *Sales and Service Excellence, Money n' Profits,* and home business magazines. His articles are published in dozens of other business and marketing journals and magazines including *Business Week Online.* He has been interviewed on radio and has appeared on *Entrepreneur* magazine's sales and marketing radio show.

Here is Charlie's story about the beginnings of his online business.

Back in the '90s he launched his first Web site. When a month or so later it wasn't showing in the search engines, he started researching how the search engines rank sites and how to put Web sites at the top. Each time he found an idea, he tested it and looked for ways to make it work even better. The result was one of the first books on how to market sites to search engines. Charlie followed this up by creating a Web site that reviewed and ranked search engines. His reference Web site "Searchiq. com" was featured on National Public Radio, in *Fast Company* magazine, as well as in *USA Today,* and it was ranked in the top 100 Web sites by *PC Magazine.* Charlie then sold this site for hundreds times more than its cost to one of the Internet's largest technology providers.

What is his motivation?

Helping others achieve the same level of success I did by applying an easy-to-use marketing strategy.

His first product and still the most popular marketing book by far on his site is *15-Second Marketing,* ironically tackling his biggest obstacle. When he first started in the '80s as a management consultant he tells us he was terrible at marketing his services. Like most small business owners, he kept trying to sell people instead of letting them sell themselves. Then he discovered a simple strategy for getting attention: building relationships and closing more sales. His business took off.

Two key traits have made Charlie a success. First, he is always looking for a better way at work and at play. After 15 years of kayaking, he is still finding ways to go faster or surf the boat and flip less frequently. When skiing he is always looking for a more efficient and fluid way to avoid the bumps and the trees. The same is true in his work. Charlie helps his clients find better ways to attract prospects and increase sales.

Second, Charlie has one core focus in his work—helping his prospects solve their marketing problems. It's this focus on client problems that is at the core of all his marketing manuals and services. Here is his advice to entrepreneurs:

Stop wasting time and money trying to reinvent the wheel. If your business needs help, get expert assistance. Too many small business owners try to become experts in everything with the result that they doom their businesses to failure. It's much more cost-effective in the long run to pay for expert assistance and use proven systems and strategies to be successful.

Northie.com

> **Name of company:** Northie Incorporated
> **Date started:** April 22, 2003
> **Web site:** www.Northie.com
> **Associate companies:** www.northiehosting.com
> **E-mail:** jshiner@northie.com

James Shiner, President of Northie Incorporated, started the business in 2003. At the time he was a junior in high school and was just trying to make some extra cash. He had been designing Web sites since 1997 and decided to turn his talent into a business. Since 2003, Northie has grown considerably, and James is now able to work full-time designing Web sites as well as offering printing services, IT solutions, and Web hosting, all while attending Suffolk University in Boston, MA.

The motivation to start my own business was the desire to work for myself. I was sick and tired of working at dead-end jobs at CVS and McDonalds, and I wanted to make money on my own, doing what I enjoyed. My girlfriend, Heather, has inspired me and helped me to develop my business, as well as taking care of all the administrative work.

My father owns his own business, so from a young age I was interested in business. My parents were big influences and motivated me to go into business for myself. They helped me when I needed help and inspired me when I needed inspiration.

My biggest obstacle was going to school full-time while running a business. Running a business is a full-time job, and at most times more than a full-time job. Sixty-hour work weeks are the norm for most business owners, especially when first starting out. Throughout my middle school, high school, and now into my college years, I have been able to maintain a balance between schoolwork and

Northie. I was able to make the Dean's List at Suffolk University while managing more than 30 Web sites of companies from all over the United States.

What are his best business traits?

- *Motivation*
- *Willingness to work hard*
- *Perfectionism*
- *Persistence*
- *Determination*
- *Understanding of business*
- *Desire to make money*
- *Skills with people*

Do NOT skimp on a Web site. Do not use the templates and "free" services. People can tell when a site is built from a template. Having a clean, professional Web site is the same as having an impressive storefront, except a Web site is seen by thousands, 24/7. Your online presence is key to success in the ever-changing business and Internet environments.

Along with making your site look good, you also need to promote it in search engines. Google has a great ad service which allows you to set a budget to spend every day, week, or month. Yahoo! has also launched a similar service. There are also sites which allow you to submit your site to thousands of the most popular search engines. But make sure your site has the correct META tags so the search engines pick it up.

Innovative Web Services

Name: Bill Baldwin

Location: Manchester, CT

Web site: www.ourmanchester.net

Type of Business: Internet marketing and Web site design

We design Web sites for small and midsize businesses and help businesses market their Web site, even if we did not design them. It's a great business. Think about what Web site design really is: well-written words and carefully selected colors and pictures. It's a great way to make a living. I tell people all the time I don't have a job, but I do work hard. A job is drudgery. Working hard is great fun.

The company was launched in January 1999. I was just laid off when the company I was working for went bankrupt. I decided I could run a company better than some of the CEOs who are running multimillion-dollar companies. So I'm giving it my best effort. I don't expect to be a multimillion dollar business owner but I don't expect to have to tell a judge, "I have no recollection of that." In other words, I run my company based on ethics.

My girlfriend, a true entrepreneur, always wanted to be self-employed so she and I started Innovative Web Services. It's been a grand circus ever since.

I love it when clients come back to me to say how much they benefit from our services. It really makes me smile when someone tells me how they gained a new client or made another sale because of the work my company did for them.

I really love my office. It's one room in a building with several other businesses. I'm on the second floor. Right outside my windows are some gorgeous trees, but the thing I love most is the squirrel that I watch having breakfast every morning.

What have been your biggest obstacles?

I have to say by far the toughest part of running my business is contacting possible new clients. I really am not comfortable making that first contact. Once I'm talking or e-mailing with someone I'm fine, but getting over that first hurdle is challenging.

Is there anything you would have done differently?

I would have learned more about marketing and sales before I started the company.

We are currently designing a series of Web sites focused on communities in Connecticut. Our plan is to go state-wide with this effort, and that will keep us busy for quite a long time. Our business model includes a piece that allows us to promote qualified nonprofits (the poorer, the better) for free, which makes us feel very good about serving the communities.

What advice do you have for others?

Learn. It's a very competitive world, and all of us need to be learning new things. Secondly, don't believe just because you are technically very good at what you do, everything will just fall into place. You really have to be working to market your business, making people aware of what you do and how it can help them.

theONswitch

Name: Nancy A. Shenker

Location: Thornwood, NY

Web site: www.theonswitch.com

E-mail: nancys@theonswitch.com

Type of Business: Marketing/PR for Start-ups and Transformations

We help businesses get off the ground and grow. We work with start-ups on all aspects of marketing: budgets, naming, branding, public relations, and Web presence. We work with established businesses that need recognition. We are not just a "creative" agency. Although we are very creative, we are obsessively focused on real business results.

I started this business in September 2003. I had spent 25 plus years in corporate marketing and felt possessed by the entrepreneurial spirit. All my previous jobs had involved start-ups and significant growth — I wanted to be able to do that full-time — and work with smaller, independent, creative businesses. I had previously worked in publishing (Matthew Bender, Prentice-Hall, Warren, Gorham & Lamont), Financial Services (Citigroup, MasterCard International), and Event Marketing (Reed Exhibitions). With start-ups at an all-time high, I decided to make the leap.

I have a spacious office in an industrial area of Northern Westchester, New York. We pride ourselves on keeping our space welcoming, inspiring, fun, and cozy. We have ample parking for guests and always have interesting fun food and exotic flavored coffee to offer them! Currently, we have three employees and a wide network of specialists who are brought in on projects

What have been your biggest obstacles?

Making the adjustment from having a corporate infrastructure to being a "do-it-myselfer" has been a challenge. I have learned to be the IT, Facilities, HR, Marketing, and Operations groups — all packed into one! And I probably would have been a bit more selective in my networking activities early on. I used to attend and volunteer for everything but have cut back to the highest-quality groups and activities.

What's the most fun part?

Whenever a client's business grows as a result of our efforts or we get a big PR "hit," I get a rush of excitement. Hearing the words, "Thank You" is always pretty cool too.

What advice do you have for others?

- *Don't be afraid to take calculated risks.*

- *Get out of your office and meet as many people as you can who can help you in various ways.*

- *If you're not loving what you do, rethink.*

Big Noise Marketing

Name: Michael Winicki

Name of company: Big Noise Marketing

Address: 834 South Union Street Olean, NY 14760

Phone: 716-373-7980

Web site: www.bignoisemarketing.com

E-mail: Mwinicki@yahoo.com

Type of Business: Small Business Consultant

I help small business owners make more money through better advertising, marketing, and operating. I've owned several businesses: consumer electronics store, florist, collection agency, pawn shop, natural food store, and business brokerage. My business experience has been a great asset. I just wrote a book, Killer Techniques to Succeed with Newspaper, Magazine, and Yellow Page Advertising. *I have put on seminars and speak regularly to groups. I've been doing consulting since 1995 and operate from a home office. There are two people in my company, and business is great!*

What has been the biggest obstacle?

The toughest part of what I do is educating potential clients on the amount of money they aren't making because of a variety of reasons—many of which deal with marketing and operations.

What's the most fun part?

The fun part is getting a phone call, e-mail, or letter from a client telling me how much more his or her sales are that month compared to the last month.

What's next on the horizon for your business?

I'm in the process of authoring more books, reports, and other aids to help small business owners.

What advice do you have for others?

Make sure you have an "angle" or a "unique selling proposition." Just don't be another "me too" business. I've worked with more than 2,000 businesses. Most fail because they do not have a unique position in the market—not because of poor cash flow.

And I'd like to thank the person who pushed me into writing my first book, Leeda McCabe.

What We Have Learned
from These Entrepreneurs

CHAPTER 5

Your Concept

The case studies of the previous section are real-life stories. These people were once just like you, making their first steps into the entrepreneurial world. Their stories should inspire, teach, and help direct you as you begin your journey. Many of the case studies presented here offer some great advice about business ownership, some of the pitfalls associated with starting your own business, and some insight into the dedication and commitment you will need.

We're also including this next section as a summarized review of the information we have learned from the entrepreneurs of the new frontier, the Internet

YOUR MINDSET

It is all about attitude! How much do you really want? Are you just dreaming? Or are you prepared to do whatever it takes to build your empire. Before you even start your business it is critical that you have the right mindset. If you think small you will remain small. If you want to be successful in business, you must think big and aim high. Don't limit yourself with thoughts of "I can't," "It's not possible," or "No one ever does that well." Yes they do! Yes you can!

What are the characteristics of the Bill Gateses and the Donald Trumps?

- They have a driving passion to succeed.
- They believe in themselves and their goals.
- They do not procrastinate. They seize the moment.
- They earn and master new techniques.
- They make strategic alliances and partner for success.
- They are not intimidated by adversities.
- They always keep a close watch on competitors.
- They are innovators, not followers.

Before you start your business, it is critical that you have the right mindset. You must have a driving passion to succeed. It is a proven fact that if you want something enough, you will find a way to attain it and break through all obstacles in your path. Start your business with success as your ultimate and final goal.

Belief in yourself and your business and goals is a must. Always believe in yourself and your business. Plan carefully and execute your goals methodically. Make a plan for one month, three months, six months, and a year. Put some thought into this and make attainable goals. Always bear in mind that different goals will have different time frames. Sometimes a goal will take a little longer but do not become discouraged. Congratulate yourself on achieving each step and adapt goals that may take a little more work and time. Remind yourself on a daily basis what you are going to achieve and decide to spend at least three hours a day working on your business. Business is not a get-rich-quick game; it requires working diligently and being smart to gain success. Always remember to work on a consistent basis; avoid working hard one day and taking off the next day. At the end of every quarter, assess your business and take a second look at your business plan. Change the goals if need be and add if necessary.

Procrastination is the reason why many fail in life. This habit can cost you your business. If you do not act on an opportunity, your competitors will. You need to be active and alert to stay ahead. In even the tightest niche there is always going to be competition, and you must be the leader. Never get left behind in the dust. Be an innovator, not a procrastinator.

Always be open to learning and mastering new techniques. Diversity is how your business will expand and penetrate new markets. When you look for new places to market and offer new products and services to your customers, you will ensure your business growth and customer loyalty.

Partnering for success is very necessary for your business. Choose your partners wisely and well. You will grow at a faster rate and truly achieve your business empire by this means.

An important part of your mindset is never to be intimidated by adversities. Like life your business will have its ups and downs; no two days are the same. However, you cannot allow yourself to get discouraged or lose sight of your goals. Donald Trump faced bankruptcy more than once, but he picked himself up every time and rose to the top again.

Here is something that many forget in their quest for success. To be a leader of the pack you must keep an eye on the rest of the wolves, namely your competitors. If you come up with a great idea, be assured your competitors are close behind ready to copy your idea.

Be an innovator, not a follower. It is the people who are not afraid to forge ahead who ultimately succeed. Learn from your competitors and create new ideas from their ideas.

When you keep a positive, think-ahead and think-big attitude, you can be the next business tycoon. If you can dream it, you can do it!

RESEARCH: MARKET ANALYSIS

Before you start to develop your product, offer, or service, it is very important to determine whether there is a market for your product or service. It will do you no good to have a great product with no market. It would be like putting up a hamburger stand in a vegetarian community. No doubt the hamburger is a good product, but the market is not interested in it. With this analogy in mind even before you develop your product, do your research on the potential markets.

Researching your market is called market analysis, the process of actively seeking out and analyzing your potential market. It is one of the critical parts of your business. Its purpose is to develop a solid marketing plan. Online is much easier than offline, as you will easily find resources to help you, and it's all at your fingertips!

Conducting Market Research

Make a list of subjects that interest you and look up each one with a keyword in Overture search tool, **www.inventory.overture.**

com/d/searchinventory/suggestion/. You will find how many people searched for your subject in the last month, and will give you an idea of how popular a certain topic/concept is. The more searches found on a topic the better your chances of selling a product within this market.

Next, look up that same keyword in a search engine **www.google. com** and you will see a number of Web sites, indicting supply. The more Web sites found, the greater your supply and the more your competition will be. Your aim is to find a well-searched topic with less supply: high demand and low supply. This will be your future niche market.

When you have decided on your market, analyze your potential customers, also known as your target market. Take a moment to think about them and ask yourself these questions:

What Web sites and messages will they visit for information? What forums and networks will they visit? Make a list of them all. These are the places you will advertise and aim your marketing. Although you cannot advertise on a forum or business network, you can post with your signature. More about this later.

What publications do they read? Make a note of these. This is where you will do your advertising.

A good plan is to make a thumbnail sketch or profile of your potential customers, using the questions and answers you found when you did your marketing analysis, research. Study the customer profile you made to find out their wants and needs. The answers you get will help you pinpoint the particular problems they are experiencing. Make a note of these. You can then get ideas to fill those needs and solve their problems with your products and services.

How do you find your niche market? Do your research for high demand and low supply markets. Do you have a unique skill or product that is hard to find? Sometimes you can identify a niche by supplying a product or service that you have found hard to get and can supply a need for others like yourself. Other times you have to penetrate a more saturated market.

Your customer base will often start with fewer people if you are a working a niche market, but you can expand your market in different ways with related products and services. If your customers like a certain product, you can also offer another one that you know will interest them. For instance, those people who like a certain golf club will also need golf balls.

Another way to create a niche in a saturated market is to add value to your service and make yourself better and different from your competitors. Added value will allow you to offer something with your service or product.

With your marketing analyses you will be able to sort out your chosen market and develop your product or service around your research findings. Then you will be ready to market your product or service.

DEVELOPMENT: YOUR PRODUCT OR SERVICE

After you have conducted your market research, you will need to develop your product or service to fit the unique needs of your target market. List the needs and wants of your market and make a note of all the products and services that would fit them. Hot ideas are:

- Info products: e-reports, e-books and instructional videos.

- A specific need: software and special tools.

- Services: match your skills to your market needs.

Info Product

- Info books and e-reports: Your best way of selling these is in digital e-book form. This is a low-cost high-profit margin. Customers like this as they can get the book as soon as they pay for it.

- Videos can be made for immediate download so they are also very cost effective after the initial cost of making the first one.

- Articles can be strong promoters of anything you are selling from your Web site. Make interesting useful articles that you can distribute and attract targeted visitors to your Web site. This is a proven way to pre-sell and make sales. They can be expanded to make high demand e-reports, which should be six to ten pages long and about a hot topic.

- Always have at least six info products to sell so that you can offer backend products. When customers have bought once from you, they have confidence and trust you so that they will buy from you again, increasing your profits without having to spend time and money on new marketing.

- If you do not have enough products, you can affiliate for some or get resale rights to some hot items. Make sure they are all related and will fit your market.

- Expand your business by penetrating new related

markets. Develop six new products and repeat your process. You will build your business quickly and efficiently.

Software

Tools to make business more efficient and easier to run are always popular. If you have programming skills to build software, they can be a good source of income. If you do not have the skills but have ideas, partner with a reliable programmer to help you build software that is in demand. Put as much information as you can on your Web site about your software product. This type of product is usually a little more costly so you must make sure the customer understands it thoroughly.

Good customer support is critical when you sell software. Most customers will have techie questions and need help using a new piece of software. Always prepare a frequently asked questions (FAQ) sheet for your customers. Set up mailers to handle initial questions so that you can quickly send your FAQ sheet to your customers.

Answer questions as quickly as possible — within 24 hours or less. Have backend products ready for sale so that you can continue to profit without having to do further marketing.

Services

Rely on your experience and expertise in a field that will interest and fill a need within your market. List all you have and match it to your market. Services are best promoted by offering valuable resources and informative content with a Web site to boost your credibility and create trust in your prospective clients. Developing a Web site when you have a service is a must and is critical to gaining new clients.

Services are based on trust and building relationships, which are achieved by having a useful, informative content-filled Web site. When you show your prospective customers your knowledge and willingness to help, they will be more inclined to hire you.

Put an inquiry form on your Web site to gather as much information as possible as soon as your prospective client sends an initial request to you.

Be prepared with an initial proposal letter, professionally written, to answer inquiries. Remember, this will be your prospects' first impression, and you want it to be a good one.

Make sure to check your grammar and spelling with every communication. Always include your professional three-line signature. This is your trademark, and it will boost your credibility.

It is critical to over-deliver with excellent customer service. Make sure you answer any queries within 24 hours or sooner. Deliver your service as quickly as possible. In the business world, time is money, and delays will cost you clients. Communication is essential. Make sure you are 100 percent sure of what your client needs before proceeding. Be prepared to work closely with your clients and ensure their 100 percent satisfaction.

WHY SHOULD THE CONSUMER BUY FROM YOU?

What is your Unique Selling Position (USP)? It is creating a position in the consumer's mind, about your company and what you are offering. The USP states your **unique position** as a company.

What makes your business different from your competitors' businesses? Study your closest competitors and see how you can be different from them. Be different, stand out from the crowd, and make sure your potential customers will sit up and take notice.

Your potential customer must have several good reasons to buy from you rather than your competitor. What added value are you offering your customers?

Selling Position

Your Company must answer the buyer's question "So what is in it for me?" It is all about BENEFITS.

Your visitors must see the overwhelming benefits of your product and services. Many companies just list features. To establish your unique selling point with your potential customers, you must list benefits not features. You must answer without a shadow of a doubt the question, "What is in it for me?"

Filling the Consumer's Need

You must convince your visitor that your product and service will fill their needs and be highly valuable to them. How do you establish your USP?

Your Sales Letter

Your sales copy must state very clearly what your unique selling position is and how your products and services will greatly benefit your reader. This will be discussed in greater detail later on.

Establish Your Brand

Branding your business makes it unique and will establish your company as a household name. You will need to consider your logo, slogan, and character or mascot.

Your Logo

This is a small graphic which represents your business. It must firmly impress on your public what your company stands for and be memorable. For instance, real estate companies often have a house silhouette incorporated into their design. Their readers know at a glance that they are in the business of buying and selling houses. Dollar signs are popular with banks and lending institutions for this same reason.

Keep your graphic simple. Use black and white or two colors only so that it can easily be put on your business stationary. Try to incorporate it into your e-mails, usually on the top of the e-mail.

Slogan

This is your business motto that people remember you by, for example, "We Do Chicken Right" by Kentucky Fried Chicken. It should be relevant and easy to remember. Your market needs to associate your slogan with your business. It will always be part of your letterhead or business card usually with your logo. Again put your slogan on every e-mail you write.

Character

Many businesses have a mascot character associated with their company to familiarize people with your company and allow them to empathize. An example would be the cartoon character of the Colonel for KFC. These characters become representatives of your company and when portrayed in every ad make your company a household name. Establishing your unique selling position is very important in your business.

- It will enable you to make a strong foundation for your sales and ad copy.

- It will establish in your customers' minds exactly what your company represents and what you can offer them.

- Branding makes your company familiar to your market and also encourages viral marketing.

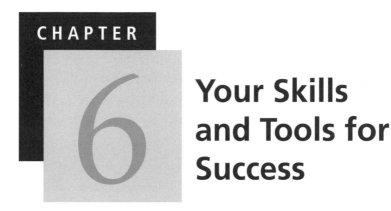

CHAPTER

6 Your Skills and Tools for Success

A large part of your success will depend upon your individual skills, assessing them and using tools to maximize them.

YOUR WEB SITE

Your Web site is your most important promotion tool for your business. Think of it as your "store front." Just as an offline business needs a store to sell products, so does your online business. Your Web site will be your selling point for your products or services. It is very important that you make a good-looking, interesting site for your visitors.

There are four main types of Web site you can build:

- Mini Web site
- Theme content Web site
- Resource Web site
- Membership Web site

Mini Web sites

Mini Web sites are just what their name implies. They are usually one or two pages, and their sole purpose is to sell, sell, sell. Typically there will be a sales page and maybe a page for affiliates. There is no attempt at pre-sell here. You will rely on an extremely persuasive sales letter. If you do not know how to write one, hire a professional copywriter—worth the money—so that you can rely on your sales page to sell your product.

Mini site #2

This will be a special page devoted to one of your affiliate programs. It is a pre-selling page and is different from the sales page. You can use it to promote all your sponsors' products or services. You can include small product reviews—honest but not gushing—to pique curiosity and get the click-through to your sponsor's page.

Theme Content Web site

To build a profitable theme Web site, you will need a central topic. If your market is health-oriented, you would have health as your main topic for your Web site. All affiliate programs, products, and services will be related to your topic and target your market.

Make a central point; a newsletter, or a tips flyer, delivered weekly or as often as you feel you can contact and build your opt-in list. There are endless possibilities. Be careful how you plan and set up your Web site. The main points for a business site are

1. Make it sticky; your visitors need to want to stay.
2. Make it load fast; do not fall into the trap of fancy graphics.
3. Make it simple; your visitor needs to find his way about; and make it focus on your products and services.

The font should be easy to read and look professional; black on a white background is best with a little use of color to emphasize your points. Be careful of capitalization and exclamation points. Never cheapen your site and credibility with too many of these.

Take a look at your competition to see how they have done it and improve.

Never give into the temptation to get a free Web site; it will cheapen your image and destroy your credibility. A little money invested will go along way to making your own personal Web site.

Resource Web site

A resource Web site is a very useful one for your visitors and when done correctly will attract large amounts of targeted traffic for your business. You can use it to promote your products, services, and to show your expertise by writing content with your resources. Or you can use it as a means of driving targeted traffic to your selling Web sites.

A membership Web site is a highly informative, value-packed site that people pay a monthly fee to use. There are many membership sites on the Internet, but few are worth the money as they are often associated with a monthly subscription newsletter.

A good membership site must:

1. **Over-deliver.** You must give your subscribers their money's worth and more. Your aim is to make sure that they will renew their monthly subscription because you are offering them a great resource.

2. **Update frequently.** Make sure you have fresh, original

content that cannot be found elsewhere. Keep up with business trends and news to keep new information constantly circulating.

3. **A forum or discussion board.** This is always good for members to discuss and answer each others' questions, and it gives you a chance to answer their questions too. In this way you will add value to your membership site.

4. **Good presentation.** This is a must since you are offering a paid product and subscribers must feel that they are getting their money's worth.

Your main objective with a membership site is retention of members. You can ensure this by over-delivering and making sure your subscribers are truly getting value for their money and more.

Your Web site is your most powerful tool. Put thought into it even before you start to build. Remember that your Web site is your business showcase or store.

YOUR NEWSLETTER

Creating Your Newsletter

Newsletters are a critical part of your business. They are how you build your enterprise into a successful company. Your opt-in newsletter subscriber base will be one of your most important business lists. A free newsletter enables you to build a list of highly targeted prospects who will become your loyal customers.

Newsletters have several functions:

- Capturing e-mail addresses for building your opt-in business list.

- Building relationships with prospects.

- Establishing you as an expert in your field.

- Allowing you to present your offers to a responsive list with a good chance to make sales.

- Making some money with third-party ads.

When visitors come to your site, they are highly targeted and are interested in the products/services you are offering. Few people buy when they have only seen your offer once. That is why it is necessary to capture their e-mail addresses and show them your offers more than once. A free newsletter is the ideal way to do this. Your autoresponder will provide you with the code to put a subscription box on your site, so that when your visitors sign up they will be automatically added to your newsletter list. Not only can you place a small ad for your main product or service, you can also offer backend products to your list.

A newsletter will allow you to build relationships with your subscribers. Try to make your newsletter an interactive one. Invite questions and answers from your subscribers and offer them a survey on what they like or dislike about the newsletter. Always answer questions in a timely manner. Give special discounts to your subscribers, make them feel special, and always treat them like the VIPs they are. Over time you will build relationships with your readers, and they will buy and use your services. In this way you will build a loyal profitable customer base.

When you write your own original articles or have them written for you, you will establish yourself as the expert in your field.

This will help you build trust and respect with your readers. As you do this, you will find subscribers will buy from you because you know about your product.

You can present your offers to a responsive list that will be more likely to buy from you, because they know and trust you. You can do surveys and find out what products and services they are interested in.

Third party ads can also make you some money with your newsletter. These are people who want to advertise to your list and will pay for advertising space inside the newsletter or for solo ads. Be careful not to send too many of these out as they annoy your readers and may cause them to unsubscribe. Make sure that these ads are offers that your readers will want and need—not unrelated products and services.

How to Make a Newsletter Effective and Allow You to Rake in the Profits

- Offer quality and be accurate.
- Use target ads.
- Do not advertise too often.
- Closely monitor third party ads.

For a newsletter to be effective, it must hold interest. Content should be worthwhile, useful, and accurate. Choose topics that they really want to know about. Make your articles original. Do not rewrite old articles or publish articles that have been around a long time. Keep your style simple and to the point. Your readers are looking for valuable information, not judging an essay on style. Make sure your information is accurate; do research if necessary. Provide free resources wherever possible and make your newsletter an enjoyable, informative read to ensure that you have the highest possible open rate and to cut down the unsubscribe rate.

As mentioned above, target your ads and make sure your advertisers are making appropriate offers for your readers. Do not advertise too often, a common mistake with publishers that loses subscribers and cut down your open rate.

BUILDING AND MANAGING YOUR LIST

There are several ways to build a targeted list.

- Ad swapping with other publications.
- Swapping subscription boxes with related businesses.
- Ad co-ops for marketing newsletters.
- Announcement lists.
- Direct advertising.
- Web site promotion.

Swapping ads with other related publications can be a good way to get targeted readers for your newsletter. People who like reading other newsletters will be interested in yours. You can do this when you have 100+ readers. Swapping subscription boxes with related Web sites will serve the same purpose.

Ad co-ops are good for quickly building a list of people who are interested in marketing tips and information on advertising. You will get a fair response rate when you target your information and ads correctly, you will give free ads to the ad co-op customers in return for their subscribing to your newsletter.

Announcement lists are also useful as many people on these lists are looking for new publications in their field and new products. Remember to read the rules thoroughly for this type of promotion.

Direct advertising can be done online and offline in publications by renting mailing lists for offline promotion.

Put a subscription box on every page of your Web site for effective Web site list building.

If you do not like to write, get a professional writer. You can find one for a reasonable price at **www.Elance.com**. The money invested will be well worth it, as over time you will build a responsive loyal list of subscribers. Over time they will start and continue to buy from you, building a profitable part of your business.

THE POWER OF INFORMATIVE ARTICLES

Article Writing and Promotion

Articles are one of the best forms of advertising and they are completely free. Now before you say, "But I can't write, and English was one of my weak points in school," stop right there and see how article writing is not the mammoth task you thought it was. Take a look at these few points and give yourself a chance. You never know what you can do unless you are willing to try something new.

Simple articles can be divided into four categories:

- An article with tips (like this one)
- Step-by-step articles

- Reviews
- General articles

An article with tips is one of the easiest to write and read. It will be made up of:

- A title that will interest the reader.
- An introductory paragraph.
- Bulleted tips or points.
- Details about those points.
- Concluding paragraph.

The title of your article is your headline and must attract your readers, so that they will want to read your article. For instance, I could have just written "How to Write an Article" you, as a reader may have said, "So why would I want to spend time writing just another article?" But I added "An Attention Grabbing Article." Now that makes the subject more interesting.

The introductory paragraph tells why writing an article is important, because you can use it as a vehicle for free advertising. Bulleted tips or points draw attention to what you are trying to tell to your readers. Details explain your points, and a concluding paragraph wraps up the ideas you have written about. You can end the paragraph with a question or statement to make your readers think about your article.

A step-by-step article will show your readers how to do something, for example "How to start a business in seven easy steps" You would use the same principles as the tip article, but instead of tips you would bullet the steps and then go into detail.

A review will be about a particular product or book giving the benefits and the flaws and your opinion. You would use the same guidelines for your heading, introduction, and conclusion. The body would not have bullets but would be written in regular paragraphs. The general articles would be written on these same guidelines.

If you follow these points you will be able to write articles and, with practice, good ones. Start with short tip articles and when you are confident go on to step-by-step. When you are really confident, go on to reviews and general articles. You will be surprised how quickly you will learn to write attention-grabbing articles.

Article Promotion

Articles can be powerful promotion tools. They are your best sales tools and can be promoted cheaply and effectively. It is important to do this right. Many people do not do article promotions correctly and are disappointed with the results.

Here are some tips for making an effective article promotion.

- Quality article
- Hot, relevant topic
- Good distribution
- Short, good bio and permission to reprint article

Quality is critical for your success. Your article must be grammatically correct and written in a readable style. It does not have to be florid or highly complex, just readable and enjoyable. Short simple sentences and paragraphs are good for your readers who are usually in a hurry.

Make sure your articles are about a topic your readers will be interested in and be curious about. Make sure it is accurate and original. You can go to the business forums to find out what the business world is talking about and what the hot topics of the day are. You then have a basis for your articles.

Distribution is very important. You cannot expect results from submitting your articles to a few places. Manual submission is free but can take a lot of time. Software can be somewhat limited. However, an actual article distribution service can be very helpful and usually not too expensive. Do your research to find out exactly what you are getting. Article swaps with other publications are free and can be very helpful.

Here is an important point, which many overlook, your bio. This can be three to six lines of 60 characters and should not sound like an advertisement. It is a concise little piece about you and your business, designed to persuade the visitor to visit your Web site. It will always include your Web-site address. You can change the bio to fit the situation you're promoting. As well as being your salesmen, articles will also boost your credibility — very important to any business, no matter what you are selling. Articles will showcase you as an expert in your field and encourage trust in your reader. Trust in your potential buyer is a large part of selling any product or service. Articles are also a large part of the learning curve when you first start a business. To run a serious business, it is critical that you are open to learning, and information articles provide the perfect media for you. A good article is short, to the point, and contains original, informative content. If you do not like writing or simply do not have the time, you can hire a ghostwriter to write an article for you. Elance. com provides a broker service to connect you to many freelance workers including writers.

Articles will create valuable links and when combined with blogs allow you to get fast inclusion into search engines.

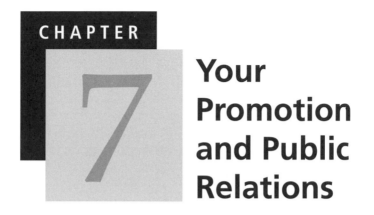

CHAPTER

7

Your Promotion and Public Relations

SALES LETTERS

Your sales letter is one of the key points for your business. It can make or break your business. You can have the best product or service but without good sales copy, you cannot sell anything. Web site visitors are becoming increasingly savvy; hype and hard selling no longer work as they used to. A subtler approach gets good results. Here are some common mistakes found in business ad copy.

- Features, not benefits
- Too much hype
- Misuse of graphics
- Using negative words
- Hard-to-read font

Listing features without clarifying benefits is a common mistake. Your prospective buyer is not interested in what a product looks like, no matter fancy it may be. He is looking for the answer to his big question: "What's in it for me?" In other words, how will the product or service you are offering help them? Will it solve an ongoing problem? Fill a pressing need? Or satisfy a yearning? Benefits will answer these questions and more.

Too much hype is a very irritating turn-off for your potential customer and can go a long way to losing the sale. Nothing is more annoying to a reader than all sorts of false promises and useless claims that cannot possibly be true. Web site visitors are educated and savvy and will not tolerate hype and blatant false claims.

Small graphics tastefully done can enhance your sales page, but try to let your words paint the picture. Large, cartoon-like graphics will bring down the credibility of your sales copy and make it slow to load. Your reader does not need to be distracted, or your persuasive sales copy will lose its effectiveness.

If you have been on the Internet for any length of time, you have heard about "Mr. Fire," Joe Vitale, a legendary copywriter and article writer. He is the master of the use of "trigger words" and subtle "hypnotic selling." What are "trigger words?" These are words that subconsciously spark a feeling of well-being and urge to buy in a reader. For example, "ramp up" your business with.... "boost" your business using this...."Discover the secret...." You have seen them. There are more than 200.

Negative "trigger words" will have the opposite effect. For example "low-income" or "failure" generates a subconscious feeling of depression and sadness in a reader and deters him from buying. People buy more when they are in an upbeat mood. Be careful how you write your sales letter or even a small ad. Words are very powerful in copywriting and will make or break the sale. As all good copywriters will tell you, selling is all about understanding your visitors' mindset.

Excessive use of punctuation, especially the exclamation point and sometimes the question mark, distracts the reader and is a turn-off for sales. Respect your reader's intelligence and do not belittle your reader with this unprofessional technique.

Too much capitalization is also unprofessional and has the same effect. Capitalization is interpreted as shouting a word. Do you want to be shouted at? I am sure this does not put you in a buying mood.

Always write with credibility in mind. It's important in persuading your prospective buyer. Unusual fonts and color combinations will take away from your sales copy and leave an unfavorable impression. Make sure the font is a normal size. Style of font should be Ariel, Times Roman, Veranda, or something similar. Do not make a sales letter in fancy type as it will distract your reader. Selling art work and cartoon drawings may be an exception to this rule.

The golden rule of making good sales copy is to write as if you are talking to a friend. Be friendly but not overly familiar. Put yourself in your reader's shoes and sell as you would like to be sold to.

AD LAYOUT AND DESIGN

Ad Design: How to Design Successful Ad Copy

To make sure your advertising campaign is effective, be very sure that your ads are written well. Good ad copy will make the difference between your ads' getting read or simply being passed over. Your ads must stand out from the crowd and reach out to your reader.

There are three basic ads in online marketing:

- Classified
- Top sponsor or middle sponsor ads
- Solo ads

Classified ads are the smallest and cheapest. They are generally placed fairly far down in an online publication and can also be used for advertising on a Web site. They do not cost very much because of their positioning and size. They make a big impact, but to do this they need to be designed effectively. Most people do not spend time on design, and their results are often disappointing, but you can turn this disappointment into success by using these tips:

- Your headline must be a "show-stopper." The reader needs to stop his browsing, sit up, and take notice.

- List a couple of benefits, just enough to excite curiosity. A classified ad makes the reader curious to go to the link and find out how he can benefit from the product.

- A classified ad presells rather than sells your product.

- Finally when your reader's curiosity is truly piqued provide the link to go to, which will bring him to your sales page.

Using Your Classified Ad

Now that you have designed your ad, write two and test which is the better sales puller. Classified ads are the cheapest form of advertising, so use them as your test copy. Whichever ad is successful, use it in as many places as you can.

You can expand your benefits and make your ads into a six- to ten-line top-sponsor ads that will be placed just before the featured article and will get good exposure inside the newsletter or Ezine. They are used for direct advertising in online publications. These ads cost a little more because of their good position and exposure. The design will be the same as the classifieds with the addition of a couple more benefits. They will produce more sales conversions than classifieds due to increased exposure.

The most expensive ads are solo ads. These are used exclusively for direct advertising with newsletters and Ezine publications. These ads are sent out to the entire database of subscribers. They can be shared sending out two together or, as their name implies, sent out alone.

Good solo ads are divided into three parts. Each part will be like a small classified ad followed by a link. They will follow the same pattern. The ad must have a good attention-grabbling headline for the whole ad, which will be the subject line for the e-mail. This must be good enough to persuade the recipient to open the e-mail. Then each of the three sections must have a good eye-catching subhead with benefits, a call for action, and a link to the sales page.

None of these types of ads is written to sell directly to the reader. This is one of the differences between offline and online advertising. Online ads will lead onto a sales page and merely warm the visitor for the sale to come. These ads should be designed for pre-selling, getting the reader to click through to the sales page, rather than selling. They must create curiosity and desire to know more from the reader, not designed for closing the sale.

Offline Classified ads

These are designed to sell your product or service. They are usually placed in local newspapers in the classified section. They can be expanded into display ads with more benefits and made into half-page or full-page ads for better exposure.

Ad design is critical to increasing your sales. If you cannot write the ads yourself, it is worthwhile to hire a professional copywriter. The money you invest will be well worth it, with the increased amount of sales you will make.

AD CAMPAIGNS: EZINE AND DIRECT MAIL

Planning Your Effective Ad Campaign

You ad campaign is a critical part of your business because its effectiveness builds your business. If you advertise only on a few randomly picked Ezines, you will have results. Advertising must be done on a regular and ongoing basis, and they involve esearch and planning.

To succeed with your campaign you need to plan and execute each step methodically. How do you do this? Here are some pointers:

- Plan your campaign. Decide where you will advertise and define your audience. Choose where you will begin your campaign and work on each area before moving to the next.

- Allocate a monthly budget that will be used only for advertising and stick to it. Start-up businesses often neglect this step, resulting in financial hardship and loss of business. Many business projects fail from lack of funds. Do not let this happen to you. Do not starve your business, but be sure to start small and work up.

- List all the ways your potential customers can be reached. Some examples are through publications they read, Web sites they visit, and discussion boards. Advertise in as many of these places as your budget allows. Your goal is to expose your business to as many places as possible. Try to penetrate every corner of your market. Find niches and do not be afraid to advertise in many different areas.

- Assess which publications are giving the best response and make a note of these. Then take your list of responsive publications and place as many solo ads as your budget allows. Run the solo ad at least two or three times for best response. Repeat the whole process for other related products and services. Note whether response is increasing or decreasing with each ad. Use more than one ad and rotate. As soon as you see response going down, switch to another product or service.

- Constantly advertise: make sure your business remains in front of your market at all times. Be sure to advertise at least once a week or a maximum of every two weeks as budget allows.

- Keep lists of opt-in prospects to advertise to. You can use mailers and e-mail marketing advertising campaigns for this purpose. Those people who have specifically asked for more information and those who have bought from you will be your opt-in lists. An example is your opt-in newsletter and your customers. Never advertise to those who have not asked for information. This is called SPAM and will get you in a lot of trouble. It can even cost you your business.

- More ways to advertise: seek out related business Web sites, swap ads with different publications, and exchange links. Try to use well-trafficked, related sites for this. Distributing articles is another effective way of advertising your business, as discussed in the previous chapter.

When you follow a plan within your budget, you can make your ad campaign efficient and successful. It will bring in small returns at first and then develop into a profitable selling machine. The golden rules are to monitor carefully, record in detail, and work methodically through each step of your campaign. Most important, never let your campaign run out of money. In this way you will build a profitable and long-lasting ad campaign.

CHAPTER

8

Web Site Development

SEARCH ENGINES, META TAGS, & SEO

Search Engines: Tips to Optimize Your Exposure

Search engines are a source of warm-ready-to-buy visitors for your Web site. They are a long-term marketing technique that will bring you increased amounts of targeted visitors. As with all marketing, research and preparation are necessary for success. They are best used when you have a broad market for your products and services. If you are working a tight-niche market, pay-per-click engines will be more effective. Prepare your submissions well because if you make a mistake or try some methods to trick the engines, you can get your Web site banned from the engines and miss out on a lot of traffic and business.

Most engines require META tags which are pieces of HTML code that some search engines rely on but most take them into consideration. META tags are not visible to your visitors but are important in getting your Web site indexed with the search engines.

There are three META tags you will need to insert into your site's HTML:

- Title
- Description
- Keywords

Search engines will use the tag to gather information about your Web site topic. The tag will appear as a hyperlink on the search engine results page and will be a way for people to click through to your site. Your title must be aimed at keyword phrase that is in your page (make the search engines happy!). It must excite curiosity to entice people to visit your Web site (make humans happy!).

Your description tag should be designed to give search engines instructions on what your page is about. It will appear on the search engine results page. It should be short and informative, no more than 13 words if possible. Put your most important information in the first few words.

Your keyword tag tells search engines what keywords they will index from your site. Only include keywords related to your site content. Be careful not to repeat a keyword more than three times, as this will harm you in the search engine response. How do people search? When people do a search they put in a keyword, briefly scan the title descriptions, and look for the most appropriate domain name. That is why it is important to put some thought into each of these META tags and your domain name choice when you optimize your Web site for the search engines.

Your Domain Name is an Important Part of Optimizing Your Site

Your domain name should have one or more of your keywords in it or preferably your keyword phrase rather than an unrelated name and it should be short. It serves two purposes. Your potential customers will associate your domain name with your product, and the search engines can index you better.

Optimized Content

For obtaining the best position in the engines you should try to put informative optimized content on your site which is informative articles that use your keywords. Both your visitors and the search engine spiders will like this type of content. You will establish yourself as the expert, and your visitors will trust you more and be willing to buy from you. Search engines also look for relevant informative content rich in keywords. A word of caution. Do not overuse your keywords in your content or the search engines will penalize you. Three percent keyword density is acceptable to the search engines.

Linking

Google is especially friendly to linking. Link to good relevant sites with only 10 links to a page and different categories. Your visitors will enjoy an extra resource, and Google will rank you higher. Blogging with links to an article can also get you into a good search engine position.

With these points you will have prepared your Web site well for the search engines. You can submit manually to them or use software to submit. If you are serious about search engine submission and plan to use the engines to get most of your traffic, you would be wise to use software tools like Web Position Gold, that will not only submit your site correctly to the search engines but will help you monitor your site's position so that you can get indexed better.

Search engines are an important part of gaining targeted Web site traffic and when entered correctly will bring in ready-to-buy customers. This will result in a steady stream of sales and help you develop your business.

AUTOMATION:
PAY-PER-CLICK, TRACKING & LINKING

When you first start your business, there are so many things to do that duties can spin out of control very quickly. To prevent problems, it is critical to automate your business whenever possible. One of your most useful tools for doing this is an autoresponder.

An autoresponder will save time and endless frustration. Its primary purpose is to help you take care of one of the most vital parts of your business, your lists. Every business accumulates business lists. Examples of these would be:

- **Multiple customer lists** — those who already bought from you multiple times and are very likely to buy again.

- **First time buyers** — those who might buy from you again in the near future.

- **Prospects or contact list** — those who are still shopping but have contacted you and need some more persuasion.

Autoresponders will take care of all these lists and more. They perform multiple tasks. Here are a few:

- Maintaining lists
- Newsletters
- Mailers

- FAQ
- Backend selling
- Thank you letters

What do we mean by "maintaining lists?" Autoresponders will automate the sign up and unsubscribe processes, automatically unsubscribe bad addresses that bounce a certain number of times, and prevent duplicate sign ups. They will inform you when people subscribe or unsubscribe from your lists, saving you hours of time, and will organize your lists into different categories.

Newsletters can be broadcast or sent out to all your subscribers, no matter how many, with one click of the mouse, saving you hours to send each one manually. Autoresponders can also preschedule your newsletter, enabling you to write it in advance and schedule it to go out at a certain time.

Mailers can be sent to your prospects. These are is a sequence of messages set up to sell a product or service sent to your list at timed intervals. The best-timed interval for information about a product or opportunity is about seven to ten days on a daily basis, and after that, every month, three months, or six months. Anyone who does not respond at all after six months is probably not interested and should be taken off the prospect list.

An FAQ list will be a set of commonly asked questions and answers. You will send it to all customers as a courtesy with your thank you note. Whenever a customer asks a question, you can have your FAQ list reply automatically with a note asking them to contact you if they did not find the answer to their questions, again saving time as the FAQ list will tackle most commonly asked questions in a timely manner.

Backend selling

This means including a small insert for a discount on a related product in one of your follow up e-mails. Customers who have bought once from you are prime candidates for future sales.

"Thank you" letters are a must for anyone who buys from you. They can be set up on your autoresponder so that as soon as a customer buys, they get an e-mail, most useful for digital products as it will include instructions for downloading your product.

Always e-mail to an opt-in-list. Each of your prospect list members are opt-ins. They must have requested information from you or subscribed to your newsletter and given you permission to e-mail them. Keep all requests and subscription letters in a separate folder to guard against SPAM complaints. Never write to anyone who has not asked you for information or subscribed to your newsletter.

Try to avoid using a free autoresponder, however tempting it may be. Free autoresponders will put their ads into your messages, making your site look unprofessional. Your credibility is very important when you doing e-mail marketing and answering your customers' or prospects' questions.

Secondly, set up a payment system that will take credit cards and automatically take payments from your customers. There are several to choose from.

Third, set up e-mail filters to send e-mails automatically to folders and junk folders, helping you organize your mail. This can be done with e-mail clients such as MSN Outlook and Endora or an autoresponder system like Mailoop.

Pay-Per-Click Google Adwords and Overture

If you want to get targeted traffic, fast pay-per-click engines and Google adwords will do this for you. Done right, this can be a cheap and effective form of advertising, but if you do not make the necessary preparations you can lose a lot of money.

Here are a few factors to consider:

- Keyword choice
- How much you will bid for a keyword
- Click conversions how much a sale is costing you
- Quality of the engine

Your keywords must be well targeted for your market and your offer. Do not make the mistake of putting in general, related words. Your wording must be specific and attract only those interested in your offer. Mass submission is the way to go – submitting 50 keywords or more by excel sheet. The pay-per-click engine you use will give you specific instructions as to how to do this. Each engine has its own special format for this. Kanoodle will help you with keywords and mass submissions when you make an account with them, a free service.

Start your bid low – five cents – and then increase to gain positions in the top 10. Remember not to bid too high as it can cost you more than each visitor is worth. Many PPCs have a bidding tool which will tell you how high the average bid is on a certain keyword and what position you will be when you bid a certain amount.

It is critical for your campaign to calculate correctly the cost of clicks per sales conversion. If you start from a basic 1 percent to 3 percent conversion of clicks to sale (one to three sales per 100 clicks) you can calculate how much 100 clicks will cost and how much you will still make per sale. You can then determine how high you can afford to bid.

Make sure you use quality PPC engines. A few good ones are Kanoodle, 7 Search, and FindWhat. Overture is not very friendly to affiliates and small businesses. Google Adwords are effective and will give you good targeted visitors and sales when done right. There are no huge deposits with Google—just $5 to start.

Pay-Per-Click campaigns are especially effective for specialized markets. With highly targeted keywords you can attract the exact person you need for your business and eliminate non-relevant visitors. Pinpointing your market is critical for your success.

Google Adwords

This is a very economical form of pay-per-click, **www.adwords. google.com**. You pay only a $5 deposit when you register and then set the amount you want to bid on each bid. Google has some good tools to help you with keywords and bidding guidelines.

Overture, now owned by **Yahoo.com**, is one of the largest pay-per-click engines. It is effective but not very friendly to small business: they do not accept affiliate programs. Kanoodle, 7Search, and FindWhat are three of the major engines that do accept affiliate programs. A work-around for affiliate programs is to make your own Web page for each of your affiliate programs or even a separate mini site.

Deposits for the search engines vary from $25 at 7Search, and FindWhat to $50 at Overture and Kanoodle. This amount is put toward your click-through, and you will be notified when you need to deposit more. Budget a certain amount per month for your pay-per-click campaigns so they do not spin out of control.

You will base your budget amount on your cost of click vs. sales conversions.

It is important to monitor your campaigns to keep them under control. Most major pay-per-click engines will include tracking with your campaign account, which is a savings. Many software tracking systems for metasearch engines also offer help with tracking. You should research keyword density and choice to avoid wasting money.

Tracking

Tracking various aspects of your business is important, allowing you to adjust your marketing streams and stay ahead of competition. Here are a few examples:

Tracking Your Ads

If you are not tracking your ads, you are losing money and valuable time. Why? Because if you do not know which ad is pulling and which have produced little or no response you could be repeating costly mistakes and missing out on valuable resources. When you know which ads are pulling, you can repeat them. Keep a log of where your successful ads are running; for example, note which Ezine for repeat advertising. If you have a similar offer that appeals to the same market, use that Ezine again. However, if an ad brings little response, make a note of this Ezine so you do not repeat similar offers. There are several programs that track ads automatically, and they are easy to set up.

Tracking Your Web Site Visitors

This can be very revealing. Most Web hosting services make this available, but if they do not, there is a Web site tracking service. Tracking your visitors will tell you which Webpage is working for you, how many visitors it takes to make a sale, which page is most profitable, and what your visitors enjoy, helping you adjust your content and Web design. You can then improve and fine-tune your site.

You Should Also Track Your Pay-Per-Click Engine Results

Most major PPC engines or services will do this for you. Always take into consideration how much each buying customer cost you by calculating the ratio of "click through" to "buy." Know which keywords are pulling. Check your bidding price on keywords and adjust it, usually by one or two cents to position yourself better. Delete those that are not getting clicks. Keep a log of all the keywords that are pulling and any sales that you have made through them. For example, there have been 100 clicks and one of them is a sale that will equal 1 percent. If you are bidding five cents per click, that sale will have cost you $5 which must be taken off your selling price. If you were charging $25 for your product, your customer has cost you $5 so your profit is $20 (less other costs). You can adjust your keyword bidding to make sure you are always profiting.

It's a good idea to put all your tracking results on an Excel spreadsheet, allowing you to compare on a weekly, monthly, quarterly, and semi-annual basis. It is very important to keep good records of your tracking results. Whether it is a small classified ad or a larger pay-per-click campaign, records are valuable for telling you exactly which ads are doing well and which are not. Ruthlessly pull out the bad ones and build on your successes. Make a note of the publications and Web sites that give you best results as well as the ones that do not. Continually test and track your ads until you have several winning ads and a list of good sites. Even when you get ads pulling customers, remember to alter the look so your readers continue to notice them.

It is necessary to advertise continually. Many people make the mistake of advertising once or twice and then giving up. It takes more than a couple of times for your readers to buy.

Track market trends. Always stay abreast of different advertising methods used in your particular field. Be assured your competitors do that. Do not be afraid to try new methods, especially with an online business, where changes can happen rapidly. Being unique and different from your competitors will pay off; your visitors will enjoy the refreshing change and be in more of a buying mood. Tracking all parts of your business will ensure your success and give you the edge on your competition.

Linking for Success

Linking to relevant sites is a powerful and free way to get many highly targeted visitors to your site. Visitors who go to sites that are similar to yours or have complementary products or services will be very interested in the products and services you are offering. They are prime prospects for your offers.

Links to other Web site can be a powerful and effective form of marketing and do not have to cost you anything, but like everything else in business they should to be done right. Here are some common mistakes and how to avoid them.

Links to Competitors

This is a common mistake. You give up potential buyers to your competitors and defeat the purpose of linking which is to increase your sales—not your competitors'.

Links to Unrelated Sites

Links to unrelated sites are not only worthless, but they will hurt your ranking with the search engines. Unrelated sites will merely bring general traffic. These people will not necessarily be interested in your offers. Google especially penalizes sites with unrelated links and those linking to link farms.

Links to Link Farms

These infamous Webmasters have hundreds of links listed in their link exchange. You will just get lost in the crowd. Links of this sort will not increase your visitors or your ranking in the search engines. Do not make link farms yourself as you will seriously hurt your ranking in the search engines and bring down your Web site value. Your visitors cannot look for resource links at your site when they are confronted with hundreds of links.

Links to Inferior Sites or Those with Little Traffic

Links to substandard sites will bring down your ranking and credibility. Be careful and picky about the sites you choose. You want to enhance your visitors' stay with valuable resources. Think of your link exchange as another valuable source of informative Web sites for your visitors.

Complementary Sites

These will give you the warm-ready-to-buy visitors you need. These sites will be happy to link to you because you are offering added value to their visitors. For instance, if you are selling golf clubs, you could link to a site selling golf balls and your mutual visitors will be interested in both your Web site offers.

Articles

One of the most powerful ways to link to others is through articles. You write a good article relating to your link partner's Web site and ask to exchange links to your site using your article. Distributing your articles to article banks and libraries will also gain you many links.

Finding Links

Look up related subjects in the search engines and choose the top 20. Look over the sites and write a letter to the owner, referencing his Web site and asking if you can exchange links with them. You should find contact information at the site. You can also use software to find linking partners or pay companies to find links for you.

Your Link Exchange

You should organize your Link Exchange into sections, all related to your market so that your visitors can find what they need easily. A well-organized directory makes you look good too. Make it easy for people to link to you. Put your contact information on your link exchange and encourage other Webmasters to link to you. Use a form to avoid SPAMmers. You can actively advertise your link exchange in publications and related Web sites, bringing you more worthwhile visitors.

With these points in mind, build your link exchange and see a steady rise in your traffic. It will not happen overnight, but you will get a steady stream of profitable visitors, at no cost, developing your business as your sales increase.

CHAPTER

9

'Networking/ Affiliate Web Sites

BUSINESS 'NETWORK FORUMS

To be successful in business you cannot afford to be isolated. Building relationships is the hallmark of a successful business. This is especially true for the Internet.

When you first go online, the World Wide Web (WWW) can be a cold, lonely place. There are many pitfalls and mystifying terms. Forums and business networks are great sources of information to help you, besides giving you good exposure. Here are some ways they can assist you:

- Get answers to your questions.

- Find customers and joint venture partners.

- Get exposure for your business.

- Provide information about the latest trends in marketing and the business world.

If you have burning questions, you can post them in a business forum and usually someone will answer and give you advice.

When you answer questions yourself and use your signature line, you establish yourself as an expert in your field. Often people will contact you for your services. Joint ventures can begin this way too. Being active on a business forum can give great exposure to your business. You can learn all sorts of things on the business forums that will keep you abreast of the trends and hot topics in the industry.

Posting comments and suggestions helps others and builds your credibility in your field. This is a nice chance to prove your worth. The Internet can be a lonely place and sometimes you feel all alone with your problems. It is nice to know there are others with the same difficulties and if you are able to help them, you feel good about yourself.

You can have your new product or Web site reviewed by other people in the forum and receive valuable feedback. There are always tech questions or even questions on how to start or market your business being posted. In this way you can get a new view on new projects or just answers to your questions. Remember

- Play by the rules.

- Use no advertising.

- Use a small two-line signature with one Web site URL.

- Be polite and respectful at all times.

- Do not get into lengthy time-consuming arguments and discussions. Your time is valuable. In business "time is money" so you do not want to spend unnecessary amounts of your time on forums. They can be very time-consuming if you are not careful.

- Answer questions whenever you can. Show your expertise and gain respect.

- Ask valid questions about business-related topics.

- You can ask for a site review but do not do this too often.

- Some forums and business networks allow posting of articles. Make them interesting, concise, and without links. Include your signature line and copyright.

If you own a newsletter or Ezine, forums are a great source of inspiration for your next article, report, or review. You will see hot topics that people are discussing and common problems businesses are having, and you can give your readers information they can use and enjoy. Readers who look forward to your issue will keep their e-mail boxes open providing you with fewer bounced e-mails.

If you have targeted visitors coming to your Web site, you may want to start a forum yourself—a nice form of marketing, too. If you have an affiliate program, an added touch is to have a discussion board or forum where affiliates can talk about their highs, lows, or ask questions. You can also introduce any new marketing techniques while answering their questions. They can interact with each other and with you. It makes for better team players and more sales in the long run for your company.

These are just a few ways you can use forums to enjoy your marketing experience. One of my favorite business forums is Anthony Blake Online located at **ablake.net/forum/index.cgi**. One that allows article posting is Ryze at **www.ryze.com**. You can find more by searching for "business forums" at Google and

Yahoo! I hope you will find time to visit the forums if you have not already done so.

AFFILIATE WEB SITES

One of the most effective ways of selling your own product or service is to have an affiliate program for your business. Once set up, it can save money and jump-start your business.

- Setting up an affiliate program.

- What your affiliates need to be successful.

- Commissions.

- Finding "super affiliates."

- Resources for promoting your affiliate program cheaply and effectively.

There are two ways you can set up your own affiliate program. You can use software like AssocTrac to track and manage your affiliate program, and it will provide a record of commissions and allow your affiliates to check their stats any time. It will also work for a two-tiered affiliate program. You can use a third party to track and record your affiliates' commissions and take care of payments. ClickBank will do this, but you cannot set up a two-tiered system with them.

Training Your Affiliates for Success

Do this as necessary, as many of your affiliates will need some help to get started. Remember, their success is your success. Here are a few ways to do this.

- Affiliate newsletter: This should be a monthly training/ tips affiliate letter.

- Set up a training center.

- Training on getting started marketing basics. Tips and information.

- Resources where to market.

- Useful Web sites and anything else that you can find to help them.

- Marketing materials: classifieds, solo ads, and articles for direct marketing and article distribution.

- Recommended reading. Encourage your affiliates to stay on top of their field.

- Always respond in a timely manner to your affiliates and answer all their questions, however trivial.

- Offer incentives when affiliates sell more of your products.

- Hold competitions every few months.

Marketing Your Affiliate Program

You can use the conventional methods like search engines, pay-per-click, and direct marketing but be sure you have good sales copy for your lead page for these forms of marketing. One of the best resource Web sites for affiliate marketing is Allan Gardyne's AssociatePrograms.com. You can advertise your associate program here.

Commissions

Make sure you have a competitive commission percentage—50 percent if possible. This will attract and keep affiliates in your program. Be sure to price your product competitively, so that both you and your affiliates will make enough money on each sale. Pay your affiliates once or twice a month on a regularly scheduled basis.

Getting Super Affiliates

For your affiliate program to succeed, you will need to attract super affiliates—people who make a good part of their living selling other people's stuff. They take their affiliate marketing very seriously and are extremely good at it. Here are a few ways to attract super affiliates:

- Search engines. Find the top ten in your field on the search engines and invite them to join your affiliate program. Make sure they have related Web sites and are not your competition.

- Use Link Popularity.com, **www.linkpopularity.com**. You can also use a useful piece of software called the Spider by Neil Shearing, **www.scamfreezone.com/spider**.

- Develop a list of the super affiliates. Visit their Web sites and write a proposal letter asking them to link with you or join your affiliate program.

- Publishers of related Ezines are good affiliates or joint venture partners.

- You can send a proposal letter to the masters of Internet marketing—the gurus.

These are just a few places you can look for affiliates and joint venture partners. Always have your affiliates' success in mind. Remember their success is your success. Make new products for them every three months, so they always have fresh products to sell.

JOINT VENTURE PARTNERS

Joint ventures. Your ultimate marketing success. You need:

- A proposal letter
- An offer that greatly benefits your joint venture partner(s)
- A contact list

A joint venture is a mutual benefit partnership. For instance, a company has software products but no way to market them. You have the marketing resources but no product. You offer your services as a marketer to the company for a commission or at a specified rate. The agreement is beneficial to both of your companies. In principle, this is how an affiliate program works, and it is called a joint venture.

The art of planning a successful joint venture is more complex than most people imagine. When you approach a publisher keep in mind that they get a number of joint venture proposals each month. Your proposal letter must be professional, respectful, and beneficial for your partner. Do not make this a straight invitation to join your affiliate program. Instead, emphasize the benefits to the publisher and their subscribers. If possible, add a valued incentive for being your joint venture partner.

Good contacts are publishers and Web site owners in your field.

As with super affiliates be sure their businesses and newsletters complement your business to make it will be a winning situation all round.

Affiliate programs coupled with joint ventures will jumpstart your business and allow you to build your company quickly and cheaply. You can get professional proposal letters written by freelance writers from Elance at **www elance.com**.

CHAPTER

10

Extra Tools, Tips, and Tricks

TAKE CARE OF YOUR BUSINESS PARTNER

Q*uid pro quo* has never been more true than in the online environment. You need the alliance and traffic that online partnerships can provide to your Web site, and in partnering with other businesses, you increase visits to your business information. Even if there are no buyers at your Web site today, visitors might remember and come back tomorrow. Linking, ad-links, SEOs, META tags, and business networking contacts are all methods you can employ to take care of yourself and your business partner.

Three Simple Tactics to Increase Sales

Sometimes when you start to market your business you fail to see the simple ways to market and instead begin with the more complex methods. Most of us start with a big advertising campaign then spend a fair bit of money doing direct advertising with many publications. This can be quite costly and not leave much money for any other types of marketing. Here are several simple, cheap, and effective ways to advertise.

A signature file, called sig line, is often overlooked as an important, free selling tool. It is a small piece of text at the bottom of each e-mail you write. Do not make this an advertisement—two or three lines about you will suffice. For example, my sig line is: Regards, Cathy Qazalbash, Freelance writer/copywriter, **www. advertise-your-business.com**. Yours should be aimed at your audience. When writing to my subscribers, I sign off with: Best wishes, Cathy Qazalbash, publisher (name of my Ezine) and the Web site address. To a client or a prospective customer I might write: Regards, Cathy Qazalbash, Freelance writer/copywriter, advertise-your-business.com. Sigs can be a powerful tool, especially if you combine them with a "PS." Readers will always notice the PS, and it brings your point across, draws attention to your signature, and tells who you are and what you do.

Article Distribution

Write, or have someone else write, some interesting articles about your business with your bio and permission for others to use the article. Either distribute them free to all libraries and directories or use a service for a nominal fee. They can be a powerful advertising tool especially if you have a service. Always be careful to copyright your work and make sure to add your bio box. Your permission for publication should be at the top and should read, "You have permission to publish this article as long as you publish it in its entirety and include the bio box."

Ad and Article Swaps

You can swap ads and articles with other publishers in related fields. This technique may not generate a lot of sales but can gain targeted subscribers. It will cost you nothing and will build your business list with valuable subscribers.

These three, simple tactics are very effective tools to advertise your business. They will help you spread the word about your company while expanding it. As more people get to know about you, your business will grow into a profitable enterprise.

EQUIPMENT

Your computer is one of your most important business partners. Considering this fact it is critical to keep your computer in the best possible condition. Your online business cannot afford any downtime. Here are the main attackers on your computer:

- Viruses
- Spyware
- Hackers (usually associated with spyware)

Viruses usually come from attachments in e-mails but can also be picked up from chat rooms, traffic surfing, occasionally from forums and even some Web sites. Bogus e-mails from PayPal, eBay, and other SPAMmers or phishers asking you to click on links within the e-mail can lure you to infect your computer. On Web sites, the links may release a virus into your system. Any type of SPAM e-mail can also be infected. It's never a good practice to click on links or open attachments that you did not solicit.

Spyware comes from a variety of sources including surfing, chat rooms, and unprotected Web sites — hackers who want to spy from your computer who download their ads and use your computer to show their ads to others. They have several ways of planting their seeds, and most often you will find the actual root of the spyware in the registry part of your computer or attached to your Web browser. This means whenever you start up your computer or open your browser you will propagate and spawn more ads for the hacker. Free downloads are common ways to transfer Spyware. Hackers planting spyware on your computer will also use different unprotected portals or windows in your internet service provider (ISP) and will be able to send ads and viruses through your computer to all your ISP customers. This can get you shut down by your ISP.

Warning signs are:

- Your computer slows down, especially on start up.
- You receive strange repetitive e-mails.
- Your e-mail system is not working properly.
- Pop ups mysteriously come up when you open a browser.
- Your browser is not functioning correctly.
- The browser is slow to open.
- Videos in your computer do not functioning correctly.
- Something does not seem quite right with your computer.

Cures and Preventions

Viruses can be held at bay by having a good antivirus software, scanning all attachments, and never opening attachments from those you do not know. Delete SPAM without even opening it and always delete your deleted e-mails as they can contain viruses. When you go to chat rooms or forums or use traffic programs, always scan your computer for viruses. If you go to unfamiliar Web sites it is wise to do a manual scan. Scan your computer regularly at least once a week, just to be safe.

A good firewall can prevent spyware and hackers; however, scan your computer at regular intervals for spyware and do not download too many tool bars as they can let it. Scan all downloads before saving them to your computer.

Taking care of your computer/partner is worth the small expense. It will save you money in the long run.

Software

You need to make the most of several key types of software.

- Software that automates your Web site and tracks your customer's habits.

- Software that enables you to design, communicate, and increase productivity.

- Software that enables you to assess and analyze the state of your business.

Each type requires you to provide input, to possess an understanding of the processes of your business, and to convey this information to the right personnel. When you begin to pull your ideas together, take the time to put together the best information management team with the best software that you can afford. It will pay off later in increased sales, satisfied customers, and larger profits for you. Software that automates your Web site and tracks your customer's habits should provide:

- Visitor information, such as age range, male, female.
- Places visited by the Internet customer while at your site.
- Mailing lists, autoresponders, and financial transactions.

Software that enables you to design, communicate, and increase productivity should enable you to:

- Create a Web site that entices the shopper to stay.
- Create powerful newsletters and ad campaigns.

Software that enables you to assess and analyze the state of your business should provide you with:

- Financial summaries
- Purchases analysis
- Customer financial profiling
- Business financial statements
- Inventory information
- Sales order tracking

Everything you undertake to accomplish via the Internet uses some type of software. You must be proficient and literate in the software world to optimize your investment.

INFORMATION MANAGEMENT

Other than the software decisions you make while in the early stages of your business's development, the greatest decision that will affect your ability to streamline and assess your business state is your choice in information management personnel.

Management of the mass of information that you acquire during the daily operations must be compiled, directed, and analyzed, or you will cost your business in lost sales and lost customers. There is also the security concern when the operations of a business online are handled improperly or without the utmost care and concern for theft of sensitive material.

An individual who can properly maintain, manage, and direct your accumulated information will prove an invaluable asset to you as well as to your business success.

Information management isn't limited only to the human element. Choosing the right software along with the right IT manager will help to ensure that your business and your information are headed in the most successful direction.

SECTION THREE

The All-Time Greats

CHAPTER 11

The All-Time Greats

As with any frontier, there are those that become larger-than-life success stories, and the same is true with the Internet Frontier. For the last section of our book, we have chosen to present some of those stories and the biographies of the individuals who have been, and in some cases still are, the driving force behind the success.

YAHOO!

Yahoo.com is one of the largest online business Web sites in the world. It was one of the first of its kind. It started with humble beginnings in the spring of 1994 by David Filo and Jerry Yang, PhD, when they were still students. They conceived it as a guide to keep track of their personal interests on the Internet, but before long they realized that they needed to make modifications and enhancements and formatted it into a categorized directory. This was the beginning of Yahoo!

They named their directory *Jerry and David's Guide to the World Wide Web*. However, they soon came up with a more interesting and appealing name, "Yahoo!" They wanted a simple directory to enable them find Web sites. Search engines were not prevalent online in 1994, and there were few if any directories to help people search. Jerry and David were pioneers in this field. Within a year Yahoo! became a busy well-used directory, celebrating its daily count of one million-visitor mark within nine months — not bad for an idea hatched by a couple of students.

Within a year Jerry and David were able to go public with Yahoo! and get others to invest $2 million in their company. This enabled them to expand and develop new services and tools for their growing base of customers without having to invest themselves, saving them money and allowing them to grow at a rapid pace.

Within two years, realizing their new company had the potential to grow quickly, they began to look for a management team. They hired Tim Koogle, a veteran of Motorola and an alumnus of the Stanford engineering department, as chief executive officer and Jeffrey Mallett, founder of Novell's WordPerfect consumer division, as chief operating officer. They secured a second round of funding in 1995 from investors Reuters Ltd. and Softbank. Yahoo! launched a highly-successful IPO in April 1996 with 49 employees. They partnered for success and hired others to spend time on management so that they could continue to develop more income streams and services.

Today Yahoo! is a multibillion-dollar enterprise and is owned by business magnate Henry Hewitt. It serves more than 345 million individuals each month worldwide. There are countless services offered by Yahoo! for free and paid for by advertisers, and they keep adding more services. Their latest are more search engine capabilities and Web hosting and domains. They have acquired Overture, one of the most widely used pay-per-click search engines, allowing them to expand their markets.

What is "Yahoo!" or a "yahoo"?

The name Yahoo! is an acronym for "Yet Another Hierarchical Officious Oracle," but Jerry and David insist they selected the name because they liked the general definition of a yahoo: "a person who is rude, unsophisticated, uncouth." Yahoo!

How Did Yahoo! Manage this Meteoric Rise to Fame?

Jerry and Dave saw an urgent need and filled it. Their timing was impeccable. There was no one offering the service, and people rushed to use it. They went public and persuaded people to invest in the business, allowing them to continue their rapid growth. They cashed in on the new online business opportunity, the Internet. There was little competition at the time they started, and they were not afraid to try something new. It paid off handsomely. They began with a small amount of money; the original directory would not have cost too much to start and maintain. Then they got investors to pay the bills, ensuring Yahoo! would always have enough money to grow.

The choice of name is also noteworthy. People can remember its peculiar and amusing name. Opening up a free gaming site and free e-mail service attracted an ever-increasing number of people to their Web site and services, giving their advertisers more exposure and encouraging more people to advertise with Yahoo! More advertisers give more revenue, and the company continues its growth. Yahoo! adds more services on a regular basis, bringing more and more people in, increasing ad revenue.

GOOGLE SEARCH ENGINE

Google is one of the largest and most sought after search engines on the Internet. Webmasters fight to gain a place within the top 10 listings. However, as with many giant companies, it started with a small idea that grew into a mighty giant in a remarkably short time. Google typifies the way a company can grow by means of the Internet, at lightning speed. An offline business can never reach such heights from scratch in such a short period.

Two students, Larry Page and Sergey Brin, founded Google in 1998. They saw a need and they filled it. They were both studying computer science and were well versed in the technology needed for their enterprise. They used their own expertise and interests to develop their product. They founded and developed a user-friendly search engine that is available in many different languages.

They made their search engine unique by adding more streams of income and incorporating a system for placing ads, called Google Adwords. These small ads are placed on millions of related Web sites and search engines by Google, and advertisers pay for the click-through received. Google, in turn, pays a percentage of its earnings to the Web sites and pay-per-click engines it uses. For Webmasters, this program is called Google Adsense. It ensures Google a never-ending supply of Web sites for its advertisers and a constant stream of advertisers who know that targeted readers will see their ads. With this advertising system, Google can afford to keep their search engine free of charge and allow free inclusion of Web sites to put into their search engine. Though there are copycats, Google can still stay ahead of them as Google is more trusted, and they continue to improve their Adwords and Adsense branches.

What makes Google a unique search engine? It allows you to find information in many different languages; check stock quotes, maps, and news headlines; look up phone book listings for every city in the United States; search billions of **images** and peruse the world's largest archive of **Usenet** messages. Google has enhanced its search engine capabilities so that they encourage more searches and can attract more paying advertisers, increasing their revenue by adding value to their product.

Recently, Google implemented a tool bar so that searches can be done easily without having to go to the Google URL. This is the ultimate convenience tool that allows people to do even more searches. It also has little tools like Form Maker that help consumers and encourage them to use the tool bar. Additional searches mean encouragement for more advertisers.

They partnered at first with Yahoo! allowing their customers to use their search engine facilities. By partnering with a potential competitor they were able to build a strong customer base quickly and easily. Even though Yahoo! has split away from Google, they can still both make money by their large reputations.

What's a Google?

"Googol" is the math term for a 1 followed by 100 zeros. The term was made up by Milton Sirotta, nephew of American mathematician Edward Kasner. It was popularized in the book, *Mathematics and the Imagination* by Kasner and James Newman. Google's play on the term reflects the company's mission to organize the immense amount of information available on the Web. Its unusual name has a great marketing value because people remember a short, funny name, and Google quickly became a household word.

How did Larry Page and Sergey Brin become so successful?

- They saw a need and filled it.

- They enhanced their product to give added benefits.

- They used their education and expertise to develop their specialty product. They built their business around something they already knew about and were interested in.

- They knew how to make multiple branches of income developing from the same product. Diversity will set your business apart.

- They knew how to make themselves different from their competitors.

- Each enhancement to their product was focused on gaining more searches for their advertisers and encouraging more customers and revenue.

- They chose an odd name that is related to their product. Theirs was the only name of that sort on the search engines when they first started, allowing them to shoot to the top of the search pages and gain targeted traffic quickly and easily.

- Their name meant searchers and customers could remember their name and helped with viral (word of mouth) advertising.

MICROSOFT

Microsoft has become a worldwide household name in a very short time, and Bill Gates is among the richest and most famous person in the world. He started the concept of Microsoft while he was still a college student, studying computer programming and using his talents to make Microsoft windows operating system. At that time it was a very simple operating system running largely on the DOS system. Over the years Microsoft was enhanced and updated until now it has become Windows XP. Microsoft was divided into a business operating system and one for home use to serve their two main markets. In 1994 the group sought to expand the support offerings to include Gopher and Web servers. This was the beginning of Microsoft explorer browser which has become one of the most widely used browsers. Microsoft added free e-mail and an ISP service to its products and its own search engine. They have a free gaming site, word processor, Office tools, and HTML editor.

No computer can run without an operating system. Bill Gates made sure he could maximize his market by developing his operating system to cater to home use and businesses. He managed to gain a monopoly over a large and expanding market and then he partnered with other friends and associates from college to form a powerful team of software and programmer experts, ensuring he could maintain and sell improved versions of his windows product and develop more programs.

He scouted his market well, appealing to the home user and business person. Word processors are vital to businesses online and offline. Again his team was able to provide updated versions to hold his market lead. His Microsoft Word has become the most widely used word processor, and he has added many other features in the Office system such as Publisher, PowerPoint and

Excel, all widely used throughout the world.

He produced an HTML editor FrontPage that was relatively simple to use ensuring his grip on the home PC users. His introduction of free e-mail and a gaming site gave him access to a huge number of people, allowed him to give his advertisers enormous exposure. He also made the Microsoft home page a news Web page that drew more people in. His latest search engine feature has increased the numbers of people exposed to MSN.

Added to this, Microsoft (or MSN) has its own Internet Service Provider which is widely used and brings in a huge income.

What made Bill Gates and Microsoft so successful?

- He saw a need and filled it.

- He used his talents and knowledge to develop a hot product that he could continue to improve and sell updated versions.

- He penetrated a large and growing market.

- He attracted huge numbers of people with free products.

- He developed related products that he could continue to sell to his markets.

- He divided his markets to expand and gain monopoly over his competitors.

- He branded his company to help make it a household name.

Filling the needs of his market

An operating system is necessary for a computer to run. At the time Microsoft was begun, the Internet was just beginning, and little competition existed for a much needed product. Microsoft easily penetrated the market and gained an edge on the competition. It ensured the market would grow at a rapid pace and sales would increase quickly. Free e-mail, free gaming site, and a search engine have been able to draw huge numbers of the general public, producing rapid growth in the market and improving sales. Once the name Microsoft became well known, new products were developed and launched quickly. All products were updated ensuring continued sales. Microsoft started with home PCs but soon penetrated the related business world and the world of home business, helping them sell even more products leading to rapid expansion.

Microsoft branding with an appealing logo, the butterfly, helped their market remember them and their company to become a household name. The name can be shortened to MSN which is easy to remember and allows easy branding.

EBAY

eBay has built an online person-to-person trading community on the Internet, using the World Wide Web. Buyers and sellers are brought together in a manner where sellers are permitted to list items for sale, buyers to bid on items of interest, and all eBay users to browse through listed items in a fully automated way. The items are arranged by topics, where each type of auction has its own category. eBay has both streamlined and globalized person-to-person trading, which has traditionally used garage sales, collectibles shows, flea markets, and local businesses, on their

Web interface, facilitating easy exploration for buyers. It enables sellers to list an item for sale within minutes of registering.

eBay is the world's largest online auction site and is among Alexa's top 100 sites. Pierre Omidyar and Jeff Skoll started it in 1995, envisioning eBay as an online market place for selling goods and services, and it has now grown to a multibillion-dollar business. In 1998 they brought in Meg Whitman to help them manage eBay. She turned the concept around, and it started to grow and expand.

First, she established the Unique Selling Point. "eBay is a company that is in the business of connecting people, not selling them things." Second, she changed the image of just auctioning collectibles and expanded the company with partnerships. She partnered with large companies that could sell their products on eBay. These partners sell large amounts of upscale items allowing eBay to make more money on transaction fees.

Today you can find anything on eBay. Despite competition from Yahoo! and Amazon, eBay continues to hold 80 percent of the auction business.

How did eBay achieve greatness?

- It fit a large market place and supplied a need.
- It adapted and changed to serve the market better.
- It partnered with large companies to obtain their business.

AMAZON.COM

Amazon is the largest bookseller online, and it was one of the first to take its offline business onto the Internet. Amazon.com,

Inc., operates Web sites that sell various products and services.

It opened its virtual doors in July 1995, starting as primarily a bookstore, but it has now branched out into multiple products and services. One of the largest online stores, the company and its affiliates operate seven retail Web sites. It also operates **www.a9.com** and **www.alexa.com** that enable search and navigation, and **www.imdb.com**, a movie database Web site.

In 1994 Jeff Bezos quit his lucrative job at a New York City investment firm, packed up and, with his wife driving, made a now legendary ride to Seattle to start what he thought would be a good business. By the time he arrived he had formed a plan to sell books on the Internet. Investors thought he was crazy, but he proved them wrong.

Jeff has always been interested in anything that can be revolutionized by computers. He saw his opportunity with the large and growing market of the World Wide Web. Intrigued by the amazing growth of the Internet, Bezos created a business model that used its unique ability to deliver large amounts of information rapidly and efficiently. Amazon.com opened its virtual doors in July 1995. The company and its affiliates operate seven retail Web sites in multiple languages.

How did Amazon.com become the huge success it is today? Jeff Bezos had a vision:

- He laid out his plan and implemented it.
- He tapped into a large growing market.
- He used his experience to start and develop his company.
- He had a high demand product.
- He expanded the business into multiple incomes.

- He was not afraid to try something new.
- He partnered for success.

Every successful business must have a plan. Jeff planned well and saw success as his only option. He envisioned success and did not let himself be stopped by negative comments. He started Amazon.com when the Internet was just getting popular so he knew that there would be growing numbers of people coming on the Internet and they would be prime prospects for his business. He forecast the growing market trend. He knew he was one of the first to tap into this market and he would get a head start on the competition. He had considerable experience about what marketing would work and what would not, allowing him to build his business quickly and get ahead of any competitors. People love information. One of the prime reasons they surf the Internet is for information. Jeff provided it at a reasonable price. A cyber bookstore meant that visitors could browse a large collection of books from the comfort of their homes. Amazon was one of the first online stores.

He has made multiple streams of income from his one idea. Amazon was at first a book store but now has everything in its retail Web sites. With multiple streams of income Jeff has managed to expand his company and keep a tight hold on his growing market. He was not afraid to try something new. Despite the fact that others thought he was crazy, he implemented his idea and showed everyone the value of originality. He has diversified — diversity makes companies successful.

He partnered with many companies to expand and develop, resulting in rapid growth. He was one of the first to have an affiliate program.

COREY RUDL

Corey Rudl will be a legend in our time in Internet marketing. Like many who start a business for the first time, he taught himself the hard way, but what made Corey different was his persistence. He made many mistakes but each time he picked himself up, learned from his failures, and forged ahead to ultimate success. His Web site, the Internet Marketing Center, is dedicated to helping all who want to succeed in Internet marketing.

He started his multimillion dollar business from his parents' basement when he was just 16 years old. This was before the Internet existed. He experimented with many forms of marketing online and offline until he found a few good ways, which brought him to success. Marketing became his passion, and he threw himself into it with a thirst to succeed.

His first big break came when he put his lifelong love of cars to work to create his first book, *Car Secrets Revealed*. After some mediocre success selling offline, he built a Web site and started to sell online. This was the best thing he ever did, he said. It was then that his hard work paid off as his book started to sell. He used the marketing skills he had learned and experimented with and made his book into a best seller. He knew he was onto something big with information books and attacked the next big market for those wanting information on Internet marketing. There was a huge, relatively untapped market when he wrote his next information book, *Insider Secrets to Marketing Your Business on the Internet*. He broke the myths and cut through the hype of all the wannabe gurus and told it exactly how it is: the things that worked and the things that do not. In it he revealed all that he had learned in his years of experience with online marketing. It was another big seller, and Corey knew he had it made.

As Corey's reputation as a true guru and master marketer continued to grow, people appreciated his honesty. His great customer service and useful information gained him a worldwide reputation. He went on to perfect his Web site, the Internet Market Center until it became a true center for Internet marketers to find information products and software to help them succeed.

Here are Corey's secrets to his success.

- He was not afraid to experiment.

- He did not let failure stop him.

- He learned from his failures and built on his successes.

- He made use of his hobby and love of cars to make a highly informative and high demand information book.

- He never stopped learning and experimenting. He made himself an expert in his field.

- He researched his markets well, found a need, and filled it. He did his marketing analysis before developing the product.

- He could convince people to buy his products and books because he was living proof that they worked. He tried them all out in his own business first.

- As Corey became famous, his competitors started jumping on his bandwagon hoping to get a piece of the pie. By keeping an eye on them, he managed to be ahead of the game so that by the time his competitors tried to mimic his products and books, he had already made his money and moved on. His reputation of always over-delivering with his products gained him loyal customers who bought from him repeatedly.

Corey Rudl's story is an inspiration to us all: it is possible to go from the basement to the penthouse, and it is within your grasp. Success is not achieved overnight, and Corey did not do it alone — he learned from others — but with hard work and persistence he made his basement operation into a multibillion-dollar empire.

ROBERT IMBRIALE

Robert Imbriale is an internet marketing expert who has helped sell more than $150 million in products and services through the Internet. He has been published internationally in more than 16 languages. Every month more than 2.5 million people worldwide read his articles that are published in thousands of magazines, newsletters, and Web sites. He is an accomplished speaker, author, and Internet marketer. He is currently president and CEO of Ultimate Wealth, Inc., a San Diego, California, based company he founded in 1999.

He started his online experience at 16 in 1984 when he bought his first computer and connected to the Internet with a service known as "Q Link" (now AOL). His computer experience at this time was a hobby. His first career was in photography, and he opened his own photo studio by the time he graduated from college in Montreal. He became a well-known commercial photographer, and as he handled large corporate accounts he became familiar with the advertising world. In 1989 he started to sell through an online bulletin board system. His first products were market research reports.

He moved to New York where he discovered his passion for

marketing and made it his permanent career. When he was just 24, he served as Director of Marketing for multimillion dollar direct-marketing firm in New York where he increased sales by more than $20 million in just 10 weeks. His successes continued until he left the corporate world in 1995.

He combined his corporate marketing skills and his love of computers to become one of the leading Internet marketers in the world. He is on both national radio and television and delivers live seminars around the country about Internet marketing. His passion for marketing and technology has been enhanced by his newfound love of psychology and personal development, which he learned to incorporate successfully into his marketing efforts. His seminars are a blend of marketing and psychology, and participants are treated to a powerful growth experience in more than just their business lives.

He is currently President and CEO of Ultimate Wealth, Inc., a San Diego, California, company he founded in 1999. He is a passionate and entertaining speaker. He has appeared on many programs including CBS Television's "This Morning," National Radio Shows like "Business Talk Radio," and "The Internet Show" on KFMB in San Diego, where he is a weekly guest. He delivers live seminars across the country and has been written up in many business magazines such as *Entrepreneur, Money Maker's Monthly*, and *Wealth Building Magazine*.

He has been described in the media as "a blend of Tony Robbins and Jay Abraham." Today he conducts live seminars, hosts regular teleconference training seminars, writes articles and books, consults with corporations of all kinds and is a much sought-after guest for radio and television programs worldwide.

How has Robert Imbriale achieved success?

- He learned from his experiences when he worked for advertising companies as a photographer. He learned about marketing and used his knowledge to build his own business.

- He developed his interest in computers and combined that with his marketing skills to develop business services and information reports. He catered to the corporate and small business markets.

- He has multiple streams of income to ensure the growth of his business.

STEVEN BOAZE

Steven Boaze started his career as a freelance writer and journalist in 1982, earning his degree part-time as he worked for a newspaper. His first journalism job was writing articles for the business section of the local newspaper. His ability to write business applications and contracts and to freelance to magazines and newspapers led Steven to venture on his own.

Steven is the chairman and founder of **Boaze.com**, Corporate Web Solutions, which consists of several businesses online and offline. He is a certified web developer and publisher of one the largest online pieces of information known today for business planning and development. He has written two successful books and more than 2230 articles featured on radio and in magazines, newspapers, and trade journals.

He started another career, beginning as an assistant and working his way up to project manager for installation and service for residential, commercial, and industrial installation of HVAC-mechanical, electrical, and plumbing with a master's license in all three trades. He has more than 29 years experience.

He is currently heading up the hurricane relief efforts for re-building the Gulf Coast as MEP Project Manager.

My Success Story by Steven Boaze:

People in business have their own different method of operation. Success for me came about the old fashioned hard way—farm life and the military. Growing up on a tobacco farm in Virginia and enduring six years of military school along with four years in the U.S. Marine Corps gave me the balance needed for survival.

In 1977 I started a second career. Construction took its place in my heart and soul while I supported my family. I started out as a helper in all areas of construction and ended up 29 years later as a project manager in the HVAC-mechanical, electrical and plumbing. Then I ventured into other areas which filled my entrepreneurial spirit, although most of my friends considered it a big mistake: it was Web development and copywriting. I already had several businesses, so this venture was certainly going to be a waste of time, they thought. Today I hardly think six figures annually is a mistake!

It's only natural that when you start a business and you are doing something different from most people that you will be considered an oddball. People told me things like: "You're not business material." "You can't make a living working for yourself." "You'll fail because nobody can ever make any money that way."

Entrepreneurship is not just about having a lot of ideas or business sense. It is also about having guts. You have to build self-confi-dence. You have to be concerned with pleasing only yourself and your Creator—not mankind. Then if you should fail with one venture, you'll just dust yourself off and start again. It doesn't matter if people think you're nuts! They aren't paying your rent and running your life. Don't be concerned with what people think you should be. Just please yourself and do what you feel is right. People are too busy competing with society and "keeping up with the Joneses" that they do things they are not comfortable with just to appease others and fit in. After failing in business, most people try to save face by telling everyone they are "just in a slump and everything will be back to normal soon." They don't want to hear: "I told you so." Unfortunately, this process only delays the problem and creates even more false hope.

If your small business is beyond repair, go out, find a job, and begin working on the next small business. Keep the family afloat and financial obligations met but look forward to the day when the new venture will succeed. Why should you try again? Simply because you won't make the same mistakes you made this time. If you built something successful before but failed, you are certain to build the next business stronger and wiser. Even if you fail the second time, it won't be because of mistakes you made the first time. You'll learn more and more and eventually be successful. It's inevitable!

NEIL SHEARING

Neil Shearing is the owner of Scamfree Ltd., **www.scamfreezone. com**. He is the author of several information e-books and countless articles.

Neil Shearing's company works hard to combat scams online, a valuable resource for consumer protection. Neil also specializes in information products and software at affordable prices. He is dedicated to helping people start and develop profitable businesses online and is always looking for new tools and resources to develop for this purpose.

He started his career as a research scientist in breast cancer. He has a PhD in the medical research field and has written several theses on the subject. However, he soon realized that his job required endless hours, leaving less time to spend with his family. Neil's entire motivation for going into business for himself is centered on his family — being able to earn a comfortable living and choose his own hours.

When he first started on the Internet about seven years ago, it was all relatively new, but Neil saw his opportunity and made his plans for financial freedom. In 1997 he started work on the **Scam Free Zone**, a consumer protection resource that tries to help combat the huge number of scams online. It's now ranked in the top 6000 Web sites for traffic, according to Alexa.com.

He started making money online with affiliate programs and while he was building money with them, he started his own Web site and newsletter, and — most important — his own product. Neil put his talents together and cashed in on the need for information products.

His first product was an information e-book written in 2001, *The Internet Success Blueprint,* taken from his real time experiences. It is a complete step-by-step guide to making and selling information e-books and truly making money on the Internet. His book was and still is a huge hit as it fulfills a great need for simple no-frills information on how to develop and sell your own product and really make a living on the Internet without spending a lot of money.

Neil used the proceeds from his book to develop more information e-books and valuable software to help business people everywhere start and develop their businesses. He also started his own membership site. By these means he had multiple streams of income to help him accomplish his goal of financial freedom.

How did he manage to sell his e-book so successfully? He started an affiliate program and got his affiliates to sell for him. As he developed more products, his affiliates jumped on the new products and duplicated their success. He continues to make money with joint ventures and new products while managing the affiliate programs that allowed him to start his business. Now he is known as a "super affiliate" and this is yet another stream of solid income for him.

Today he has achieved his financial goals and lives comfortably with his wife and children in Devon, England. He has time to enjoy his family and freedom to set his own hours.

Neil's success is due to several factors:

- He had a positive goal, not a pie-in-the-sky dream: financial freedom and time to spend with his family.

- He wanted to get out of his grueling research job enough to work hard on his business, no matter what the setbacks and succeed.

- With his scientific training he made a plan, set his goals, and worked methodically to achieve them.

- He used his talents and developed his skills to ensure success. He made sure that he read and acquired the knowledge to build his business.

- He is not afraid to try new products and avenues.

- He partnered with skillful trustworthy programmers to develop his software. If you do not have a skill, partner with those who do to achieve your goals.

- He works smart, not hard, to achieve true financial freedom. Neil uses cutting-edge technology to automate his business so that he no longer has to spend hours on it and he can still make a comfortable living.

Neil has no dreams of making a six-figure income; his goal is to make a comfortable living and have the freedom to do what he wants when he wants. This is exactly what he has done.

JAY CONRAD LEVINSON

Jay Conrad Levinson is the Chairman of Guerrilla Marketing International, a marketing partner of Adobe and Apple. He has served on the Microsoft Small Business Council and the 3Com Small Business Advisory Board. His Guerrilla Marketing consists of a series of books, audiotapes, videotapes, an award-winning CD-ROM, newsletter, consulting organization, and Web site. It offers a way for you to spend less, get more, and achieve substantial profits.

With more than 30 years' creative advertising and marketing experience, Jay Conrad Levinson is a legend in the marketing field. He is the author of the best selling marketing series of all time, *Guerilla Marketing Excellence* and *Guerilla Marketing Online.* Jay shows how to spend less and make more by using unconventional ways to serve existing customers and build business through repeat sales and referrals. His strategies include 100 guerilla marketing weapons any company can implement tomorrow; how to outperform your competition using imagination and energy instead of brute force and enormous marketing budgets; how to identify niche markets, build promotional partnerships, create easy referral programs, generate hot leads; and the 12 keys to a successful marketing attack.

He has also written 30 other business books. His Guerrilla concepts have influenced marketers so much that today his books appear in 39 languages and are required reading for many MBA programs worldwide. He taught guerrilla marketing for ten years at the extension division of the University of California in Berkeley, and he was a practitioner of it in the United States as Senior Vice-President at J. Walter Thompson, and in Europe, as Creative Director and Board Member at Leo Burnett Advertising. He is a prolific writer and writes monthly columns for *Entrepreneur* magazine, articles for *Inc.* magazine, online monthly columns on the Microsoft Web site, and occasional columns in *The San Francisco Examiner*. He also writes online columns regularly for **Onvia.com**, **FreeAgent.com**, **MarketMakers.com**, and **InfoUsa. com** in addition to columns for **Guru.com**.

He has assisted many businesses with their advertising, including help with branding, the most famous being the "Marlboro Man" for Marlboro cigarettes. He is a strong motivational speaker and is in great demand for live events.

What has made Jay Conrad Levinson the success he is today?

- He educated himself and used his experience working in the advertising business to develop a unique marketing system.

- His Guerilla Marketing system can be adapted and used in any business offline and online.

- His product is in high demand.

- He appeals to a wide market.

- He has multiple streams of income.
- He partnered with others to expand and develop.

First, Jay educated himself and became an expert in his field. He used his valuable experience in advertising to develop his product. His marketing system was unique and he managed to capture a niche market in a very competitive field. His Guerilla Marketing took his market by storm and became an in-demand product. It can be adapted to any business online and offline, making it even more desirable. His product is appealing to a very wide and growing market.

Jay has developed several sources of income: coaching, information business books, and speaking engagements. He is able to expand into new markets to ensure the stability and ongoing development of his company. He partnered and joint ventured with other marketers and writers to produce more information books and sell more products and services. He is an innovative marketer who is not afraid to try new things. With his vast experience in his field he can pinpoint profitable marketing techniques.

DR. JOE VITALE

Joe Vitale is the world's first hypnotic marketer. He is President of Hypnotic Marketing, Inc., and author countless information, marketing, and copywriting books, including the number one best-selling book, *Spiritual Marketing*, the best-selling e-book *Hypnotic Writing*, and the best-selling Nightingale-Conant audio program, *The Power of Outrageous Marketing*. He is founder of the world-famous hypnotic marketing concept.

When he first began, Joe was broke and certainly not the successful man we know today, but he discovered his talents. One of his first information books was *The Seven Lost Secrets of Success* written in 1995. He is a certified hypnotherapist, a certified metaphysical practitioner, a certified Chi Kung healer, and an ordained minister. He also holds a doctorate in Metaphysical Science and another doctorate in marketing. He used his training as well as his talents to launch a series of best-selling information books on marketing and copywriting. He has now become one of the top copywriters in the world, and one of the most successful, respected, marketers.

He developed hypnotic marketing, and he wrote a successful book called *Hypnotic Marketing*. This marketing appeals to the readers' subconscious thinking and sells by means of special hypnotic words that compel them to buy. Joe uses his training as a hypnotherapist to press his readers' "hot buttons" and increase sales.

He is a busy inspirational speaker who has addressed hundreds of business groups. One association, "The Speakers Platform," rated Joe as one of the top 25 speakers in the world on sales and marketing. Joe now does executive mentoring as well as lecturing, writing information books, and copywriting.

He has studied marketers from the early 1900s until current day, and has mastered the art of merging old, modern, and future marketing concepts to create some of the greatest marketing methods in the world.

How did Joe Vitale get to be successful?

- He used his inner talents and training.
- He created a niche within a very competitive market.

- He multiplied his streams of income.
- He never stops learning.
- He is not afraid to experiment.
- He partners with and forms good business relationships.
- He remains focused and works meticulously with clients.

He found talents he could use to start his business; he combined them with his training to write best-selling information e-books. In this way he found something that interested him and that he loved to do making it easier to spend the long hours necessary to build his business. When you enjoy something you will find it easier to do, he said.

He created a niche market in a very competitive field. With his hypnotic marketing, Joe created an original form of marketing. A niche market is very important in a business, as it allows you to specialize in your market and get ahead of your competition. Joe's methods are unique allowing him to reach his market before his competition.

He multiplied his streams of income. He not only wrote books but started to put his methods into practice with his copywriting and marketing service. Now he gives lectures and seminars and offers an executive mentoring service. By having multiple streams of income, Joe makes sure he is always making money.

He never stops learning. His rise to fame can be attributed to the meticulous research that he did on marketers from the 1900s onward. He continues to learn and keep up with trends and techniques in his field to ensure that he remains the foremost expert in his field.

He is not afraid to experiment and because he tries and tests different techniques in marketing he is able to stay ahead of his competition. Businesses thrive on originality. This is how they can penetrate new markets and stay ahead as leaders in their field. He has partnered with many authors to write new books and do joint ventures, allowing him to inject new material into his books and sell more. Joint ventures and partnerships will also allow you to expand your business at next to no cost.

He remains focused and works meticulously with clients. "My work is my love so it's a joy to do," he said. He obeys the golden rule of service: love what you do and enjoy working for your clients. In this way he will make sure that his clients are 100 percent satisfied, and he will enjoy working with them.

DR. KEN EVOY

A Canadian physician, Dr. Ken Evoy is a well-respected Internet marketer throughout the world and has written many highly-acclaimed information e-books. He is the creator of **Site Build It**, a revolutionary site builder, designed to make small business owners successful on the Internet.

Ken was born in Montreal in the early '50s. His doctorate is in Anatomy and Medicine from McGill University in Canada. Originally he had no intention of becoming an entrepreneur.

In 1983 he and his wife started selling ideas and inventions for new toys and games. As the Internet became popular, Ken began to experiment with his hobby — penny stocks — and learned first hand what worked and what did not on the Internet. After much labor, his Web site on this subject became very popular. He put all his findings together and wrote a best-selling information ebook called *Make Your Site Sell* (MYSS). At first he sold his book at a low price of $17. He undercut all his competitors and revealed many proven methods of successful marketing, drawn directly from his own experience.

What really made the book stand out from other courses and similar e-books is that it offers a vast amount of information and its extremely low price. The success came not just from the huge amount of information, more than 800 pages, with a depth of expert knowledge, but also from the price Ken charges for his course. Whereas most courses of that size cost several hundred dollars, Ken still sells his course for under $50.

But Ken did not stop there. He developed a comprehensive Web building system known as *Site Build It* or SBI as it is now most commonly known. This is a user-friendly, Web building, promotional system for online business that even the newest person to Internet business world can understand.

Ken has published many information books on different aspects of marketing on the Internet and is constantly working on new developments for *Site Build It*. His own daughter makes a good living using his tools and methods.

What has made Dr. Ken Evoy so successful?

- He used his scientific training to experiment until he found out which successful Web promotion methods worked.
- He developed products that were in high demand.
- He used a penetrating price to sell his first products.
- He has excellent customer service.
- He uses his own tools to be successful.

- He has multiple streams of income.
- He uses free samples as a powerful promotion tool.
- He has automated his selling and promotional system.

Ken made use of his scientific training to find out what works and what does not, and he used proven methods to help him achieve success. His information products and his Web building system are in great demand. Ken has a large and growing market of people wanting to start a small business using Web site promotion.

His prices are reasonable and very affordable for those wanting to start a business on the Internet. In fact, he undercuts most comparable products in the market. Anyone using Ken Evoy's products and tools is aware of his outstanding customer service and support that give added value and make his products more desirable. More people will recommend his products and he has gained further success through word of mouth marketing.

He openly uses his own tools and products for his own business. He has multiple streams of income from his site building system and his information books and courses. He uses free samples to promote his products, a powerful pre-selling tool. He relies solely on his affiliates to make sales and does not actively promote his products anymore. This ensures that his selling system is automatic, saving him a lot of time.

MARC JOYNER

Mark Joyner is the CEO of **aesop.com** and one of the early pioneers of Internet marketing. He is a frequent guest expert on national television and radio. Formerly a U.S. Army officer and cold war veteran of U.S. Army Intelligence, he turned his fledgling one-man Internet business from a shoestring budget into a multi-million dollar international corporation.

He is responsible for creating many of the top 100 most visited sites in the world and has helped other sites achieve this status as well. He speaks Korean fluently, plays guitar, sings for a Los Angeles band, does his best thinking "hanging upside down in inversion boots," lives in a Hollywood apartment that was once the home of Errol Flynn, surfs the beaches of Southern California ("poorly," he adds), works out two or three times a day, is involved in various philanthropic activities, and can be found chatting with panhandlers on the streets of Hollywood from time to time ("for my benefit, not theirs," he said).

In 1995, his multibillion dollar empire started humbly as a one-man "basement operation." He used his background in military tactics to develop a very different approach to marketing. He started with a newsletter while still in the army and built a valuable business list over the years. One of his earliest ventures was the traffic program, StarBlaze, which he operated when traffic programs were in vogue. He wrote information books on marketing and business, one of the most famous being *Mind Control Marketing*. This book sums up most of his marketing methods drawn from his army days. Marc was always a controversial innovator, but his originality paid off. By the time he left the Internet, his company, **Aesop.com,** was worth millions.

His company developed useful products and software for Web promotion and development, among them ROIBot. A unique and useful software, it was user friendly, inexpensive, and available to the novice or experienced entrepreneur. Much of his wealth and success were due to the strategic partnerships and joint ventures he made, particularly with Jay Conrad Levinson in the Guerrilla Marketing project. He was and still is a highly sought-after seminar speaker.

How did Marc Joyner achieve success?

- He used his army experiences to implement a unique approach to marketing.

- He developed and used a large, valuable business list with his newsletter.

- He developed software and products that were original and reasonably priced.

- He catered to a growing market.

- He had multiple sources of income.

- IIe was not afraid to experiment.

- He made controversy part of his marketing strategy.

- He practiced innovative marketing.

He was always an innovator who stayed ahead of the competition and was one of the leaders in his field. He merged conventional methods with original ones and developed brand new techniques in his market.

His software products were unique, useful, and affordable for his market. He knew what his customers wanted and made sure he was the first to develop them. He catered to start-up and developing businesses, a huge and growing market. He developed a large number of information books, software, tools, and programs to help his market, and he speaks publicly. He made sure his business had multiple streams of income. He was always experimenting and was not afraid of failure. His writing purposely provokes controversy, as Marc knew this is a big draw when selling. His crowning achievement was his development of a large subscriber list for his newsletter, enabling him to negotiate many profitable joint ventures and sell his products to his subscriber list.

ALLAN GARDYNE

Allan Gardyne is the owner of the **AssociatePrograms.com**, an affiliate programs directory and has been earning a good living from affiliate programs since 1998.

He began his career as a journalist and started his affiliate resource site in 1998 because he could not find any such directory for affiliates. He knew he had a great "in-demand" product. It took him a little time to develop the business, but once others started to know about the new resource Web site it became very popular. Today Allan's affiliate directory has become a valuable resource site for all affiliates.

He also developed another site, **PayPerClickSearchEngines.com,** a useful resource about pay-per-click engines, a very effective and cheaper form of promotion advertising. Many successful affiliates have done well with this form of promoting. This Web site is in high demand for Alan's market.

Today he is very successful making money from a few affiliate programs and the programs he promotes on his two resource Web sites. He lives in the quiet backwoods of Australia with his wife and can now enjoy the freedom that a successful business brings.

He is a super affiliate himself and fully understands his market and what resources they need. He is always learning and has studied many marketing books. He put his learning to good use as he developed and marketed his resource sites. One of the biggest reasons for his success has been his partnership with others, enabling him to do many joint ventures promoting his Web sites. Viral marketing from his partners and visitors and his newsletter's strong following have also contributed to his success.

Allan Gardyne's success secrets:

- His products are targeted to his market.
- He used his skills as a super affiliate to teach others.
- He is always learning.
- He has partnered for success.

He was one of the first to develop a directory especially for affiliates. He duplicated that success by developing one for pay-per-click engines as well. He made a hot-selling product that would attract huge numbers of visitors from his targeted market.

With his knowledge of affiliate marketing he is able to teach others to use his proven methods. He has set himself up as a trusted expert in his field. This ensures that his visitors will trust him enough to join with him in his affiliate programs and click through to his sponsor's sites to buy.

He has read widely and continues to learn about his business and new promotion methods. Ongoing learning can ensure that your business will continue to grow and prosper. Alan always has the needs of his market in mind. He has made many friends and has partnered with them for joint ventures to promote his business. Joint ventures are a powerful and cheap way to promote your business through just one partner. Alan has brought 50,000 visitors a month to his site.

PHIL WILEY

Phil Wiley lives out in the scenic mountains of Australia. He makes his living almost entirely by working affiliate programs. Many people say that it is impossible to earn a decent living from these programs, but Phil has proved them wrong. He developed a unique method of marketing them by putting up a mini site for each of his affiliate programs that he promotes separately.

Added to that, he runs a newsletter with a large list for marketing his affiliate products and tools. He wrote a best-seller that teaches people how to duplicate his success.

His success story is simple:

- He developed a unique marketing method.
- He has multiple streams of income.
- He has a large responsive newsletter.

His unique marketing method is easily duplicated and can be used for multiple affiliate programs in many different markets. He is never tied to one market and can expand into any market that has a good affiliate program. His sites are not complicated to set up and are easy to maintain.

With his mini site system he can automate his business and spend fewer hours working to gain financial freedom. These sites enable him to have multiple streams of income and to diversify.

With his large, responsive newsletter he can continue to sell his affiliate products to his list and also find out which ones are most effective. His success can be measured by his smart use of mini sites to automate and expand his business.

Glossary

Source for terms and definitions: **www.marketingterms.com**

LINKING STRATEGY

Link checker: Tool used to check for broken hyperlinks.

Deep linking: Linking to a Web page other than a site's home page.

Inbound link: A link from a site outside of your site.

Outbound link: A link to a site outside of your site.

Reciprocal links: Links between two sites, often based on an agreement by the site owners to exchange links.

INTERNET ADVERTISING DEFINITIONS AND TERMS

The following definitions about Internet advertising terms and definitions will give you a better understanding of some of the many Web advertising concepts you need to learn so that you can successfully advertise on the Internet.

Source for terms and definitions:
http://searchcio.techtarget.com/sDefinition/
0,,sid19_gci211535,00.html

Ad rotation: Ads are often rotated into ad spaces from a list. This is usually done automatically by software on the Web site or at a central site administered by an ad broker or server facility for a network of Web sites.

Ad space: An ad space is a space on a Web page that is reserved for ads. An ad space group is a group of spaces within a Web site that share the same characteristics so that an ad purchase can be made for the group of spaces.

Ad view: An ad view, synonymous with ad impression, is a single ad that appears on a Web page when the page arrives at the viewer's display. Ad views are what most Web sites sell or prefer to sell. A Web page may offer space for a number of ad views. In general, the term impression is more commonly used.

Ad: For Web advertising, an ad is almost always a banner, a graphic image, or set of animated images (in a file called an animated GIF) of a designated pixel size and byte size limit. An ad or set of ads for a campaign is often referred to as "the creative." Banners and other special advertising that include an interactive or visual element beyond the usual are known as rich media.

Advertising network: A network representing many Web sites in selling advertising, allowing advertising buyers to reach broad audiences relatively easily through run-of-category and run-of-network buys.

Affiliate marketing: Affiliate marketing is the use by a Web site that sells products of other Web sites, called affiliates, to help market the products. Amazon.com, the book seller, created the first large-scale affiliate program and hundreds of other companies have followed since.

Banner: A banner is an advertisement in the form of a graphic image that typically runs across a Web page or is positioned in a margin or other space reserved for ads. Banner ads are usually Graphics Interchange Format (GIF) images. In addition to adhering to size, many Web sites limit the size of the file to a certain number of bytes so that the file will display quickly. Most ads are animated GIFs since animation has been shown to attract a larger percentage of user clicks. The most common larger banner ad is 468 pixels wide by 60 pixels high. Smaller sizes include 125 by 125 and 120 by 90 pixels. These and other banner sizes have been established as standard sizes by the Internet Advertising Bureau.

Beyond the banner: This is the idea that, in addition to banner ads, there are other ways to use the Internet to communicate a marketing message. These include sponsoring a Web site or a particular feature on it; advertising in e-mail newsletters; co-branding with another company and its Web site; contest promotion; and, in general, finding new ways to engage and interact with the desired audience. "Beyond the banner" approaches can also include the interstitial and streaming video infomercial. The banner itself can be transformed into a small rich media event.

Booked space: This is the number of ad views for an ad space that are currently sold out.

Brand, brand name, and branding: A brand is a product, service, or concept that is publicly distinguished from other products, services, or concepts so that it can be easily communicated and usually marketed. A brand name is the name of the distinctive product, service, or concept. Branding is the process of creating and disseminating the brand name. Branding can be applied to the entire corporate identity as well as to individual product and service names. In Web and other media advertising, it is recognized that there is usually some kind of branding value, whether it is an immediate or delayed response. Companies like Proctor and Gamble have made a science out of creating and evaluating the success of their brand name products.

Caching: The storage of Web files for later re-use at a point more quickly accessed by the end user.

Cache server: In Internet advertising, the caching of pages in a cache server or the user's computer means that some ad views won't be known by the ad counting programs and is a source of concern. There are several techniques for telling the browser not to cache particular pages. On the other hand, specifying no caching for all pages may mean that users will find your site to be slower than you would like.

Click rate: The click rate is the percentage of ad views that resulted in click-throughs. Although there is visibility and branding value in ad views that don't result in a click-through, this value is difficult to measure. A click-through has several values: it's an indication of the ad's effectiveness, and it results in the viewer's getting to the advertiser's Web site where other messages can be provided. A new approach is for a click to result not in a link to another site but to an immediate product order window. What a successful click rate is depends on a number of factors, such as the campaign objectives, how enticing the banner message is, how explicit the message is (a message that is complete within the banner may be less apt to be clicked), audience/message matching, how new the banner is, how often it is displayed to the same user, and so forth. In general, click rates for high-repeat, branding banners vary from 0.15 to 1 percent. Ads with provocative, mysterious, or other compelling content can induce click rates ranging from 1 to 5 percent and sometimes higher. The click rate for a given ad tends to diminish with repeated exposure.

Click stream: A click stream is a recorded path of the pages a user requested in going through one or more Web sites. Click stream information can help Web site owners understand how visitors are using their site and which pages are getting the most use. It can help advertisers understand how users get to the client's pages, what pages they look at, and how they go about ordering a product.

Click: According to ad industry recommended guidelines from FAST, a click is "when a visitor interacts with an advertisement." This does not apparently mean simply interacting with a rich media ad, but actually clicking on it so that the visitor is headed toward the advertiser's destination. It also does not mean that the visitor actually waits to fully arrive at the destination, but just that the visitor started going there.

Click-through: A click-through is what is counted by the sponsoring site as a result of an ad click. In practice, click and click-through tend to be used interchangeably. A click-through, however, seems to imply that the user actually received the page. A few advertisers are willing to pay only for click-throughs rather than for ad impressions.

Co-branding: Co-branding on the Web often means two Web sites or Web site sections or features displaying their logos (and thus their brands) together so that the viewer considers the site or feature to be a joint enterprise. Co-branding is often associated with cross-linking between the sites, although it isn't necessary.

Cookie: A cookie is a file on a Web user's hard drive (it's kept in one of the subdirectories under the browser file directory) that is used by Web sites to record data about the user. Some ad rotation software uses cookies to see which ad the user has just seen so that a different ad will be rotated into the next page view.

Cost-per-action: Cost-per-action is what an advertiser pays for each visitor who takes some specifically defined action in response to an ad beyond simply clicking on it. For example, a visitor might visit an advertiser's site and subscribe to its newsletter.

Cost-per-lead: This is a more specific form of cost-per-action in which a visitor provides enough information at the advertiser's site, or in interaction with a rich media ad, to be used as a sales lead. Note that you can estimate cost-per-lead regardless of how you pay for the ad. In other words, buying on a pay-per-lead basis is not required to calculate the cost-per-lead.

Cost-per-sale: Sites that sell products directly from their Web site or can otherwise determine sales generated as the result of an advertising sales lead can calculate the cost-per-sale of Web advertising.

CPA: See cost-per-action.

CPC: See cost-per-click.

CPM: CPM is "cost per thousand" ad impressions, an industry standard measure for selling ads on Web sites. This measure is taken from print advertising. The "M" has nothing to do with "mega" or million. It's taken from the Roman numeral for "thousand."

CPS: See cost-per-sale.

CPTM: CPTM is "cost per thousand targeted" ad impressions, apparently implying that the audience you're selling is targeted to particular demographics.

CTR: See click-through rate.

Demographics: Demographics is data about the size and characteristics of a population or audience, for example, gender, age group, income group, purchasing history, and personal preferences.

FAST: FAST is a coalition of the Internet Advertising Bureau, the ANA, and the ARF that has recommended or is working on guidelines for consumer privacy, ad models and creative formats, audience and ad impression measurement, and a standard reporting template together with a standard insertion order. FAST originated with Proctor and Gamble's Future of Advertising Stakeholders Summit in August 1998. FAST's first guideline, available in March 1999, was a guideline on "Basic Advertising Measures." Our definitions in this list include the FAST definitions for impression and click.

Filtering: Filtering is the immediate analysis by a program of a user Web page request in order to determine which ad or ads to return in the requested page. A Web page request can tell a Web site or its ad server whether it fits a certain characteristic such as coming from a particular company's address or that the user is using a particular level of browser. The Web ad server can respond accordingly.

Fold: "Above the fold," a term borrowed from print media, refers to an ad that is viewable as soon as the Web page arrives. You don't have to scroll down (or sideways) to see it. Since screen resolution can affect what is immediately viewable, it's good to know whether the Web site's audience tends to set their resolution at 640 by 480 pixels or at 800 by 600 (or higher).

Frequency cap: Restriction on the amount of times a specific visitor is shown a particular advertisement.

Hit: A hit is the sending of a single file whether an HTML file, an image, an audio file, or other file type. Since a single Web page request can bring with it a number of individual files, the number of hits from a site is a not a good indication of its actual use (number of visitors). It does have meaning for the Web site space provider, however, as an indicator of traffic flow.

House ad: Self-promotional ad a company runs on its media outlets to put unsold inventory to use.

Impression: According to the "Basic Advertising Measures," from FAST, an ad industry group, an impression is "The count of a delivered basic advertising unit from an ad distribution point." Impressions are how most Web advertising is sold and the cost is quoted in terms of the cost per thousand impressions (CPM).

Insertion order: An insertion order is a formal, printed order to run an ad campaign. Typically, the insertion order identifies the campaign name, the Web site receiving the order and the planner or buyer giving the order, the individual ads to be run (or who will provide them), the ad sizes, the campaign beginning and end dates, the CPM, the total cost, discounts to be applied, and reporting requirements and possible penalties or stipulations relative to the failure to deliver the impressions.

Inventory: Inventory is the total number of ad views or impressions that a Web site has to sell over a given period of time. Usually, inventory is figured by the month.

IO: See insertion order.

Keyword marketing: Putting your message in front of people who are searching using particular keywords and key phrases.

Media broker: Since it's often not efficient for an advertiser to select every Web site it wants to put ads on, media brokers aggregate sites for advertisers and their media planners and buyers, based on demographics and other factors.

Media buyer: A media buyer, usually at an advertising agency, works with a media planner to allocate the money provided for an advertising campaign among specific print or online media (magazines, TV, Web sites), and then calls and places the advertising orders. On the Web, placing the order often includes requesting proposals and negotiating the final cost.

Opt-in e-mail: Opt-in e-mail is e-mail containing information or advertising that users explicitly request (opt) to receive. Typically, a Web site invites its visitors to fill out forms identifying subject or product categories that interest them and about which they are willing to receive e-mail from anyone who might send it. The Web site sells the names (with explicit or implicit permission from their visitors) to a company that specializes in collecting mailing lists that represent different interests. Whenever the mailing list company sells its lists to advertisers, the Web site is paid a small amount for each name that it generated for the list. You can sometimes identify opt-in e-mail because it starts with a statement that tells you that you have previously agreed to receive such messages.

Pay-per-click: In pay-per-click advertising, the advertiser pays a certain amount for each click-through to the advertiser's Web site. The amount paid per click-through is arranged at the time of the insertion order and varies considerably. Higher pay-per-click rates recognize that there may be some "no-click" branding value as well as click-through value provided.

Pay-per-lead: In pay-per-lead advertising, the advertiser pays for each sales lead generated. For example, an advertiser might pay for every visitor who clicked on a site and then filled out a form.

Pay-per-sale: Pay-per-sale is not customarily used for ad buys. It is, however, the customary way to pay Web sites that participate in affiliate programs, such as those of Amazon.com and Beyond.com.

Pay-per-view: Since this is the prevalent type of ad buying arrangement at larger Web sites, this term tends to be used only when comparing this most prevalent method with pay-per-click and other methods.

Proof of performance: Some advertisers may want proof that the ads they've bought have actually run and that click-through figures are accurate. In print media, tear sheets taken from a publication prove that an ad was run. On the Web, there is no industry-wide practice for proof of performance. Some buyers rely on the integrity of the media broker and the Web site. The ad buyer usually checks the Web site to determine whether the ads are actually running. Most buyers require weekly figures during a campaign. A few want to look directly at the figures, viewing the ad server or Web site reporting tool.

Psychographic characteristics: This is a term for personal interest information that is gathered by Web sites by requesting it from users. For example, a Web site could ask users to list the Web sites that they visit most often. Advertisers could use this data to help create a demographic profile for that site.

Rate card: Document detailing prices for various ad placement options.

Rep firm: Ad sales partner specializing primarily in single-site sales.

Reporting template: Although the media have to report data to ad agencies, media planners, and buyers during and at the end of each campaign, no standard report is yet available. FAST, the ad industry coalition, is working on a proposed standard reporting template that would enable reporting to be consistent.

Rich media: Rich media is advertising that contains perceptual or interactive elements more elaborate than the usual banner ad. Today, the term is often used for banner ads with pop up menus that let the visitor select a particular page to link to on the advertiser's site. Rich media ads are generally more challenging to create and to serve. Some early studies have shown that rich media ads tend to be more effective than ordinary animated banner ads.

ROI: ROI (return on investment) is "the bottom line" on how successful an ad or campaign was in terms of what the returns, generally sales revenue, were for the money expended (invested).

RON: See run-of-network.

ROS: See run-of-site.

Run-of-network: A run-of-network ad is one that is placed to run on all sites within a given network of sites. Ad sales firms handle run-of-network insertion orders in such a way as to optimize results for the buyer consistent with higher priority ad commitments.

Run-of-site: A run-of-site ad is one that is placed to rotate on all nonfeatured ad spaces on a site. CPM rates for run-of-site ads are usually less than for rates for specially-placed ads or sponsorships.

Self-serve advertising: Advertising that can be purchased without the assistance of a sales representative.

Splash page: A splash page (also known as an interstitial) is a preliminary page that precedes the regular home page of a Web site and usually promotes a particular site feature or provides advertising. A splash page is timed to move on to the home page after a short period of time.

Sponsor: Depending on the context, a sponsor simply means an advertiser who has sponsored an ad and, by doing so, has also helped sponsor or sustain the Web site itself. It can also mean an advertiser that has a special relationship with the Web site and supports a special feature of a Web site, such as a writer's column, a Flower-of-the-Day, or a collection of articles on a particular subject.

Sponsorship: Sponsorship is an association with a Web site in some way that gives an advertiser some particular visibility and advantage above that of run-of-site advertising. When associated with specific content, sponsorship can provide a more targeted audience than run-of-site ad-buys. Sponsorship also implies a "synergy and resonance" between the Web site and the advertiser. Some sponsorships are available as value-added opportunities for advertisers who buy a certain minimum amount of advertising.

Targeting: Purchasing ad space on Web sites that match audience and campaign objective requirements. Techtarget.com, with over 20 Web sites targeted to special information technology audiences, is an example of an online publishing business built to enable advertising targeting.

Underdelivery: Delivery of fewer impressions, visitors, or conversions than contracted for a specified period of time.

Unique visitor: A unique visitor is someone with a unique address who is entering a Web site for the first time that day (or some other specified period). Thus, a visitor who returns within the same day is not counted twice. A unique visitors count tells you how many different people there are in your audience during the time period, but not how much they used the site during the period.

User session: A user session is someone with a unique address who enters or reenters a Web site each day (or some other specified period). A user session is sometimes determined by counting only those users that haven't reentered the site within the past 20 minutes or a similar period. User session figures are sometimes used, somewhat incorrectly, to indicate "visits" or "visitors" per day. User sessions are a better indicator of total site activity than "unique visitors" since they indicate frequency of use.

View: A view is, depending on what's meant, either an ad view or a page view. Usually an ad view is what's meant. There can be multiple ad views per page views. View counting should consider that a small percentage of users choose to turn the graphics off (not display the images) in their browser.

Visit: A visit is a Web user with a unique address entering a Web site at some page for the first time that day (or for the first time in a lesser time period). The number of visits is roughly equivalent to the number of different people who visit a site. This term is ambiguous unless the user defines it, since it could mean a user session or it could mean a unique visitor that day.

SEARCH ENGINE MARKETING

Description tag: An HTML tag used by Web page authors to provide a description for search engine listings.

Doorway domain: A domain used specifically to rank well in search engines for particular keywords, serving as an entry point through which visitors pass to the main domain.

Doorway page: A page made specifically to rank well in search engines for particular keywords, serving as an entry point through which visitors pass to the main content.

Invisible Web: The portion of the Web not accessible through Web search engines.

Keyword: A word used in a performing a search.

Keyword density: Keywords as a percentage of indexable text words.

Keyword research: The search for keywords related to your Web site, pinpointing the ones that yield the highest return on investment (ROI).

Keywords tag: META tag used to help define the primary keywords of a Web page.

Link popularity: A measure of the quantity and quality of sites that link to your site.

Link text: The text contained in (and sometimes near) a hyperlink.

Log file: File that records the activity on a Web server.

Manual submission: Adding a URL to the search engines individually by hand.

Meta tag generator: Tool that will output META tags based on input page information.

Meta tags: Tags to describe various aspects about a Web page.

Pay-per-click search engine: Search engine where results are ranked according to the bid amount, and advertisers are charged when a searcher clicks on the search listing.

Search engine optimization: The process of choosing targeted keyword phrases related to a site, and ensuring that the site places well when those keyword phrases are part of a Web search.

Search engine submission: The act of supplying a URL to a search engine in an attempt to make a search engine aware of a site or page.

Search spy: A perpetually refreshing page that provides a real-time view of actual Web searches.

Title tag: HTML tag used to define the text in the top line of a Web browser, also used by many search engines as the title of search listings.

Top 10: The top ten search engine results for a particular search term.

URL: Location of a resource on the Internet.

Volunteer directory: A Web directory staffed primarily by unpaid volunteer editors.

SEARCH ENGINES AND WEB DIRECTORIES

Search engine: A program that indexes documents, then attempts to match documents relevant to the users' search requests.

Metasearch engine: A search engine that displays results from multiple search engines.

Portal: A site featuring a suite of commonly used services, serving as a starting point and frequent gateway to the Web (Web portal) or a niche topic (vertical portal).

Web directory: Organized, categorized listings of Web sites.

AltaVista: Search engine located at **www.altavista.com**.

Ask: Metasearch engine located at **www.ask.com**.

DogPile: Metasearch engine located at **www.dogpile.com**.

Excite: Portal located at **www.excite.com**.

Fast Search: Search syndication company located at **www. fastsearch.com** and **www.fast.no** — also powers the search engine located at **www.alltheweb.com**.

Go Network: Defunct portal located at **www.go.com**.

Google: Search engine located at **www.google.com**.

Goto: Pay-per-click search engine that changed names and is now located at **www.overture.com**.

Inktomi: Search syndication company located at **www.inktomi. com**.

Ixquick: Metasearch engine located at **www.ixquick.com**.

Looksmart: Web directory located at **www.looksmart.com**.

Mamma: metasearch engine located at **www.mamma.com**.

MSN Search: Search destination at **search.msn.com**.

Northern Light Search: Search engine located at **www.northernlight. com**.

Raging Search: Search engine located at **www.raging.com**.

Yahoo!: Portal located at **www.yahoo.com**.

Zworks: Metasearch engine located at **www.zworks.com**.

WEB DESIGN AND MARKETING

Ad space: The space on a Web page available for advertisements.

ALT text: HTML attribute that provides alternative text when non-textual elements, typically images, cannot be displayed.

Animated GIF: A graphic in the GIF89a file format that creates the effect of animation by rotating through a series of static images.

Bookmark: A link stored in a Web browser for future reference.

Cascading style sheets (CSS): A data format used to separate style from structure on Web pages.

Favico: A small icon that is used by some browsers to identify a bookmarked Web site.

Flash: multimedia technology developed by Macromedia to allow much interactivity to fit in a relatively small file size.

Frames: A structure that allows for the dividing of a Web page into two or more independent parts.

Home page: The main page of a Web site.

JavaScript: A scripting language developed by Netscape and used to create interactive Web sites.

Linkrot: When Webpages previously accessible at a particular URL are no longer reachable at that URL due to movement or deletion of the pages.

Navigation: That which facilitates movement from one Web page to another Web page.

Shopping cart: Software used to make a site's product catalog available for online ordering, whereby visitors may select, view, add, delete, and purchase merchandise.

Site search: Search functionality specific to one site.

Splash page: A branding page before the home page of a Web site.

Web browser: A software application that allows for the browsing of the World Wide Web.

Web design: The selection and coordination of available components to create the layout and structure of a Web page.

Web site usability: The ease with which visitors are able to use a Web site.

ABOUT THE AUTHOR:

Rene' Richards is a published author and writer of business and finance articles for readers across educational and entrepreneurial boundaries. She and her family live in rural Alabama where she is a practicing accountant and financial services advisor.

Index

More Great Titles from Atlantic Publishing

DESIGN YOUR OWN EFFECTIVE EMPLOYEE HANDBOOK: HOW TO MAKE THE MOST OF YOUR STAFF: WITH COMPANION CD-ROM

Our Employee Handbook Template is the ideal solution to produce your own handbook in less than an hour. The companion CD-ROM in MS Word contains the template that you can easily edit for our own purposes; essentially fill in the blank. The book discusses various options you may have in developing the policies. Our employee handbook has been edited and approved by lawyers specializing in employment law. Developing your own handbook now couldn't be easier or less expensive! 288 pages.
Item # GEH-02 $39.95

365 ANSWERS ABOUT HUMAN RESOURCES FOR THE SMALL BUSINESS OWNER: WHAT EVERY MANAGER NEEDS TO KNOW ABOUT WORKPLACE LAW

Finally there is a complete and up-to-date resource for the small business owner. Tired of high legal and consulting fees? This new book is your answer. Detailed are over 300 common questions employers have about employees and the law; it's like having an employment attorney on your staff. Topics include: equal employment opportunity, age discrimination, Americans with Disabilities Act (ADA), unacceptable job performance, termination, substance abuse, drug and alcohol testing, safety, harassment, compensation policies, job classifications, recordkeeping, overtime, employee performance evaluations, wage and salary reviews, payroll and much more. 288 pages.

Item # HRM-02 $21.95

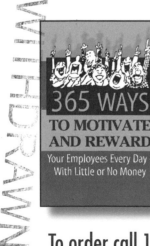

365 WAY TO MOTIVATE AND REWARD YOUR EMPLOYEES EVERY DAY—WITH LITTLE OR NO MONEY

This book is packed with hundreds of simple and inexpensive ways to motivate, challenge, and reward your employees. Employees need constant re-enforcement and recognition—and here's how to do it. You will find real-life, proven examples and case studies from actual companies that you can put to use immediately. You can use this book daily to boost morale, productivity, and profits. This is your opportunity to build an organization that people love to work at with these quick, effective, humorous, innovative, and simply fun solutions to challenges.   **288 Pages • Item # 365-01 • $24.95**

To order call 1-800-814-1132 or visit www.atlantic-pub.com